D1547206

"Constantly Risking Absurdity"

X

"Constantly Risking Absurdity"

The Writings of Lawrence Ferlinghetti

by
Michael Skau
University of Nebraska at Omaha

The Whitston Publishing Company
Troy, New York
1989

Library of Congress Catalog Card Number 87-50835

ISBN 0-87875-353-2

Printed in the United States of America

Contents

Acknowledgements

I wish to express my appreciation to my parents, my brothers and sisters and their families, my friends and colleagues, particularly Professor Susan Rosowski and Dr. Missy Dehn Kubitschek, who have encouraged me and patiently endured my interests, and to my students who have shared my enthusiasm. I also thank Professors Edward Brandabur and Cary Nelson at the University of Illinois, who directed my dissertation on the Beat Generation writers. In addition, the University of Nebraska at Omaha has granted me valuable research support. I also appreciate the assistance provided by the following libraries: the Bancroft Library at the University of California, the Rare Book and Manuscript Library at Columbia University, the Humanities Research Center at the University of Texas, the Kenneth Spencer Research Library at the University of Kansas, and the Interlibrary Loan staff at the University of Nebraska at Omaha. Finally, I would like to express my gratitude to Lawrence Ferlinghetti, whose writings over the past thirty years have provided me with delight, pleasure, and inspiration.

I acknowledge credit to the following periodicals, which publisher earlier versions of three chapters of this book:

Concerning Poetry 20 (Summer 1987): 57-71;

Critique: Studies in Modern Fiction 19.3 (April 1978): 40-46. Reprinted with permission of the Helen Dwight Reid Educational Foundation. Published by Heldref Publications, 4000 Albemarle St., N.W.,Washington, D. C. 20016. Copyright © 1978.

Modern Drama 22.1 (March 1979): 29-38.

I also offer gratitude to the following for permission to reproduce copyrighted materials:

Lawrence Ferlinghetti, *A Coney Island of the Mind.* Copyright © 1958 by Lawrence Ferlinghetti. Reprinted by permission of New Directions Publishing Corporation.

The *Engagé* Stance

O but we dreamed to mend
Whatever mischief seemed
To afflict mankind....
—"Nineteen Hundred and Nineteen"—W. B. Yeats (206)

Many of the Beat Generation writers prided themselves on their refusal to encourage any form of political alignment. Lawrence Ferlinghetti is among the most avowedly political in subject matter, a stance which he claims made him appear heretical in Beat circles: "But I am put down by Beat natives who say I cannot be Beat and 'committed' at the same time" (Jacket notes). His involvement, he asserts, is involuntary: "Politics is a drag, but every once in a while you get dragged into it and have to sound off" (Meltzer 135-36). Similarly, in a 1965 interview, he explains, "Politics is a big drag. I'm getting further away from it, not closer to it. . . . satire and politics keep creeping in whenever a situation exists that I get angry about" (*Idiot* 17). The book-length *Tyrannus Nix?* (1969), most of the "Public & Political Poems" of *Open Eye, Open Heart* (1973), *A Political Pamphlet* (1976), and the protest poems of *Who Are We Now?* (1976) and *Landscapes of Living & Dying* (1979) testify to the recurrence of those situations which goad the *engagé* writer into violating his resolutions to muffle the political voice. Ferlinghetti has written poems on virtually every issue which has become politically prominent since the mid-1950s: the Cuban revolution, the war in Vietnam, atomic and nuclear armaments, racism, civil disobedience, overpopulation, drug abuse, and threats to the ecosystem. These poems include his "broadsides," which Ferlinghetti describes as "satirical tirades—poetry admittedly corrupted by the political, itself irradiated by the Thing it attacks" (quoted on *Starting* back cover). Consequently, he employs a visceral, populist attack on the impersonal, omnivorous structures of bureaucracy and nationalism, and he celebrates "the power of poetry to transcend all the boundaries of the world dividing people from each other" (*Seven Days*) and the humane ideals which exalt absolute freedom of behavior, opportunity, and expression.

The measure of invisible domination by contemporary government can be gauged by the nature of the critical response of the artists. Consciously or unconsciously following in the footsteps of Alfred Jarry, twentieth-century artists have resorted to a peculiar form of "pataphysics" (defined by Jarry as "the science of imaginary solutions"),[1] whereby the images of control are subjected to grotesque personal abuse and vitriolic caricature. Jarry's portraits of Ubu are clear examples, as are the savage drawings of George Grosz. Salvador Dali's *Premonition of Civil War* and Pablo Picasso's *Guernica* image a similar quality through violent biomorphism and physical distortion. A related temper drove the Surrealists to value the Marquis de Sade for his political philosophy. More recently, the spirit that informed Lenny Bruce's political routines, Stanley Kubrick's *Dr. Strangelove*, Barbara Garson's *Macbird*, Philip Roth's *Our Gang*, the impersonations of recent presidents on *Saturday Night Live*, and Gary Trudeau's comic strip *Doonesbury* also shares this ambiance. For many twentieth-century artists, political criticism via craft and imagination is no longer designed to address issues but to excoriate personalities. Its politicking is not that of the editorial but that of the political cartoon; in fact, in many newspapers *Doonesbury* appears on the op-ed (opinion-editorial) pages rather than on the comic pages. Ferlinghetti's situation affords significant parallels: notes on the back cover of his collection *Landscapes of Living & Dying* point out that "most of these poems have already appeared on the Op/Ed pages or in the news sections of major metropolitan dailies, and this fact alone makes the book unique among new poetry collections." However, these forums do not necessarily temper the approaches or views of the creative talents appearing there: implications, projections, and fantasies often replace analysis as the attacks become visceral rather than cerebral. This constitutes a popular rather than professional response to the helplessness which the common people share. The political arena seems filled with specialists who may or may not feel compelled to reveal information to the public because the propagation of public ignorance is crucial to governance. The response of the artists to this predicament is not appreciably distant from the apathy of the people: all feel that nothing can be done. The artists, in exasperation and desperation, do not resort to a journalistic counting of the dead; instead they shower the figureheads of power with their enraged abuse.

Ferlinghetti clearly lies within this spectrum. Compelled by conscience to articulate his distress over the misuse of power, he nevertheless recognizes a futility in politically motivated artistic endeavors. Asked in an interview, "How vital do you think it is for a poet to express a deep political commitment?" Ferlinghetti indicates the ambiguity of the poet's situation: "It's very important but lately I've come round to the view that it's better for the poet to write a letter to the editor if he wants to write poetry that's going to mean anything ten years later" (*Riverside* 3). The topical, sometimes even occasional, nature of political satire threatens artistic creation with obsolescence. Janel Mueller points to some critical elements in the approach:

> Political poetry steeps itself in its own occasion. . . . When, as often, it also plunges a reader into a welter of specific references, topical weight compounds with a programmatic burden that seems to threaten accessibility and interest if not the status of this poetry as art. Can political poetry be justified as poetry? It looks at first as if it can, if we draw a few qualitative distinctions. Versified or not, propaganda remains propaganda, but this fact has no bearing on the poetic treatment of social values and social choices. Lines crammed with names and catchwords may reduce to journalism without entailing that circumstantiality and public events are unfit materials for poetry. (475)

Ferlinghetti himself comments on the limitations involved:

> For instance, what's the use of reading my poem, "A Tentative Description of a Dinner to Impeach President Eisenhower," [sic] today? It was a satirical poem which was only effective at the time. A few months ago, I wrote one titled "Where's Vietnam?" [sic] which is a satirical tirade on President Johnson as Colonel Cornpone, and this will be dead in no time. (*Idiot* 17)

The poet even questions the immediate effects of protest art: "This new book of mine that New Directions put out, *Tyrannus Nix* [sic], they printed a lot of copies, but what is it going to change? It is not going to change anything, it seems to me" (Meltzer 143). In a later interview, he tempers this pessimism with awareness of the writer's responsibility to commitment, no matter how negligible: referring to *Seven Days in Nicaragua Libre*, he says,

> You mean writing the book about Nicaragua? Well, that's the only thing we can do. We don't have control of the mass media, television for instance. All we can do is our little number, which in our case is writing books which don't have mass circulation. It's just a drop in the bucket. (*Beef* 4)

Contrary to Ferlinghetti's own denigration of them, the best of his satirical tirades hold up remarkably well as affecting and complex statements of enduring values. What weaknesses they possess result from the fact that details, particularly allusions to elements of popular culture and to the personal idiosyncrasies of public figures no longer in the spotlight or headlines, rapidly become dated trivia.

Aiming for what he calls "a new commensensual 'public surface'" ("Populist Manifesto," *Who* 63), Ferlinghetti loads his poems with allusions to and details derived from the popular mass media. He announces at the beginning of *Tyrannus Nix?* that "Nixon Nixon bush league President this is a *populist* hymn to you and yours" (1; emphasis supplied), and a similar characterization could be applied to his other tirades. As a result, slogans from bumper stickers and posters, brand names and jingles and catchphrases from advertisements and commercials, lyrics from popular songs, quotes from political rallies and the press, allusions to best sellers—all forms of Americana—become ingredients in the poet's populist potpourri. He employs phrases

> floating around in the people's minds from advertising or some slogan and I give them a little twist. I was always trying to write so that the poems could have a public surface which any one can get, but there's no reason it couldn't have another level which only the instructed can get. (quoted by Gleason)

This bi-level structure helps keep the allusions impervious to the transience of fads and fashions and to the brief life of advertising slogans. Thus, a reader from a different culture or a later generation can discover contextual meaning for the passage "Is there a tiger in the tank" (*Tyrannus* 10) without awareness of the Esso gas slogan "Put a tiger in your tank." In this case, the allusion adds resonance rather than meaning to the poem—

although one cannnot ignore the possibility that Ferlinghetti is blaming commercial interests for military aggression. The phrase "My country tears of thee" from "Junkman's Obbligato" (*Coney* 54 and 57), which reappears in "A World Awash with Fascism and Fear" (*Open* 87), develops significantly with one's recognition of its allusion to the familiar American patriotic song.

Ferlinghetti also highlights the idiosyncrasies and behavior of his targets, as they have been popularized by the mass media's attention to the personalities of political figures. For example, the Eisenhower administration provided an early focus for satire:

> and an inaudible Sunday bomb
> > > fell down
> catching the president at his prayers
> > > > on the 19th green
> > ("In a surrealist year," *Coney* 14);

> . . . while deep in the heart of South America the President's left-hand man was proving all the world loves an American;
> . . . the Great Soldier had become the Great Conciliator who had become the Great Compromiser who had become the Great Fence Sitter. . . . ("Tentative Description of a Dinner to Promote the Impeachment of President Eisenhower," *Starting* 41; 42)

Ferlinghetti disavows an intent of personal abuse while at the same time revealing his vulnerability to the charge:

> Well, I hope all these people see that ["Tentative Description . . . Eisenhower"] is not aimed at Mister Eisenhower personally but at The President. He is a Real Nice Man. Just like Dad. Trueblue. Just not too bright in his President's uniform. It's just like the real nice man inside the cop's costume—you may hate the uniform for the power of the state it represents, but the man inside is not *it*. He's just a deluded walking symbol of it. (Jacket notes)

Similarly, near the end of *Tyrannus Nix?* Ferlinghetti confides to the Nixon he has been lambasting: "This really isn't addressed to you It's a curse and a cry to any old President or any old general or any assassin or lover who happens to be running things by the time this is printed" (72-73). However, the personally directed nature of the specific details in the satirical tirades seems to belie such a disclaimer. In modern literature, as Samuel Charters points out,

> The most successful political poems using contemporary techniques
> seem to be personal poems, satirical or insulting, even offhand,
> with their point of reference to the place where the political
> irritation rubs against them. (80)

Name calling, exaggeration, and insinuation become staples of Ferlinghetti's polemic. Ronald Reagan is characterized as "The Gunfather," "the Tall Cowboy," and "the Great Smiler" (*The Gunfighter*; "Tall Tale" 1 and 2); Jimmy Carter is "the Great Charmer" ("Tall Tale" 1); Lyndon Johnson is cast as "Colonel Cornpone" (*Tyrannus* 43; "Parade Tirade" and "Where Is Vietnam?" *Open* 74 and 77-78); Richard Nixon is variously called "Old Tricky Dick," "Old Swivelhead," and "Old Flappy Tongue" (*Tyrannus* 19, 37, and 64). In fact, *Tyrannus Nix?* comprises a clangorous crescendo of abusive tones. Like the political cartoonist, Ferlinghetti depends heavily on physical distortion: Nixon is caricatured as "the face we all love in the Geritol ads," having a "hogjaw jughead mask" and an "Ed Sullivan smile" (*Tyrannus* 2, 17, and 40). Names of the poet's targets are also susceptible to ridicule: "Eisenhoover is dead" (*Tyrannus* 37); Ferlinghetti plays allusively with Nixon's first name: "Old Lionhearted" (*Tyrannus* 5) and "Richard Poor Richard this is your Almanach" (*Tyrannus* 14). At times the indictments arrive in such a flurry that allusions mix incongruously: "The Vietnam albatross still hanging heavy 'round your neck oh Uncle Ahab" (*Tyrannus* 23). The author's vision loses any semblance of objectivity and reality as it stares in fascination through the distorting glasses of imagination. Bawdy jokes and vulgar insinuations share perspectives with legitimate criticisms. A speculation seduces the speaker into the creation of a routine, similar to those of Lenny Bruce and William Burroughs, which then rides through the frontiers of fantasy and absurdity. Like Pope's bitter condemnations of Sporus and Atticus in "Epistle to Dr. Arbuthnot," Ferlinghetti's political criticism comes to depend upon parody and invective.

If this is what Ferlinghetti, in "Letter to a Young Poet in Cuba or Maybe Spain," calls "la voce del popolo" (*Open* 86), the voice is that of an enraged (or perhaps inebriated) populace. Its embittered coarseness springs from frustration and futility. In his "Translator's Note" for a volume of Jacques Prévert's poetry, Ferlinghetti makes a statement that applies equally well to himself:

> Prévert (as Picon put it) is the voice of the wise street-urchin—
> precocious, mocking, bitter, dupe of nothing and no one. He is even
> compared to Daumier for the way he unmasks and deflates judges,
> generals, presidents, popes and academicians—all those he thinks
> keep us from joy. (4-5)

The stance is that of "the little guy," the common person who feels himself bullied, manipulated, and victimized by controlling powers unconcerned with, even oblivious to, the general welfare. Ferlinghetti is pleased to be addressed as *Compañero* rather than *Camarada* in Nicaragua: the former word for him "has always had a touch of the fields in it, of poor provinces, of the earth itself" (*Seven Days*). This generalized humanity is the audience for which Ferlinghetti aims. As a populist writer, he values immediate clarity as a primary goal. He explains,

> I read Carl Sandburg, Edgar Lee Masters, Vachel Lindsay, and
> other Populist writers. This early Populist influence is reflected in
> the *Populist Manifesto* I wrote in 1975. I liked the way these
> writers communicated directly. None of them was obscure. (quoted
> in Cherkovski 24-25)

The danger of such directness is that the poet may become essayist, didactic and prosaic. Again, Ferlinghetti's comments on Prévert are pertinent: "At his best he simply shows you something and lets you draw your own conclusions. At his worst he draws them for you with too maudlin a touch . . ." (3). Ferlinghetti himself has not entirely escaped this preachiness. As though distrustful of the perspicacity of his readers, he sometimes becomes hortative, spelling out his materials letter by letter. For example, in "A World Awash with Fascism and Fear," his criticism is pedantically and verbosely detailed, telling rather than showing:

> And this land runneth over with fascism
> > underground & overground
> > not to mention Scientology
> > > and its psychic authoritarianism
> > not to mention one branch of the followers of
> > > Gurdjieff the Baron Munchausen of the mystics
> > and his psychic authoritarianism
> > not to mention certain aspects of Synanon
> > > whose Leader must have once read
> > > Hermann Hesse's *Bead Game* and seized upon it
> > > as the perfect model for a self-contained élite

> society within a society
> with its own hierarchy its own peer groups
> and its own compleat morality
>   not dependent on the Outside World
> Not to mention certain psychedelic
>   marathon encounter groupies
> and their psychic authoritarianism
>   in the Inside World
> Not to mention the Inside-out world
> of great non-fascist governments
> which can't exist without supporting
>   fascist paradises around the world
> Let us not go into that. (*Open* 89-90)

Let us not indeed. The apophasm of the phrase "not to mention" suggests that the poet's instinct was true, but his magisteri-
al concerns lead him into a discursive list of violations which
lacks the sparks of imagistic energy. Commenting on Ferlinghetti's "Adieu à Charlot," Robert Peters suggests that the poet's
"stark didacticism . . . is made palatable by Ferlinghetti's fresh-
ness, humor, and intelligence" (25). However, Ferlinghetti's
catalogs of villainous elements are not always redeemed by these
qualities. Furthermore, poetry should not need to depend on
the values Peters cites in order to counterbalance decided
weaknesses. In fairness, however, one must also recognize that
Ferlinghetti, evidently aware of the artistic weakness of such
directness, has revised sections of his poems to eliminate the
problem. In the original City Lights publication of "One Thous-
and Fearful Words for Fidel Castro," Ferlinghetti included a sar-
castic passage about columnists who were critical of Castro:

> and are also qualified to call him Communist
>   with a capital C
> because they know the difference between Soviet Communism
>   (which put the "slave" back in Slavic)
>   and socialism with a small c.

When the poem was later included in the collection *Starting
from San Francisco,* the passage was omitted.

The bluntness of Ferlinghetti's approach makes mani-
festly visible the subjects of his criticism: the oppressive and
destructive forces which he believes dominate contemporary
society. His themes focus primarily on violence, nationalism,
and capitalism. In "Salute," a mock paean, he cites a series of

purveyors of violence, ranging from the civilian level of "every hunter with rifles mounted in pickup trucks" to the national and international levels of "any and all who kill & kill & kill & kill for Peace," and concludes with a bitter, vulgar tribute: "I raise my middle finger / in the only proper salute" (*Open* 79-80). One of his most moving poems, "Assassination Raga," mourns the deaths of John F. and Robert Kennedy and recognizes that "The force that drives the bullet / through the gun / drives everyone" (*Secret* 5). The Dylan Thomas echo underscores the pervasiveness of violence in a world where pain and death are regrettably part of the inevitable scheme. Most serious, however, is the poet's concern over the threats of atomic and nuclear warfare. Larry Smith points out that Ferlinghetti has a powerful biographical connection with this danger: during his U. S. Navy service in 1944, he visited Nagasaki six weeks after the atomic bomb was dropped there. Ferlinghetti comments on what he witnessed: "You'd see hands sticking out of the mud . . . all kinds of broken teacups . . . hair sticking out of the road—a quagmire—people don't realize how total the destruction was" (quoted in Smith 14). In "Endless Life" this human and material destruction escalates in the poet's vision into a grim anticipation of a "World upon a mushroom pyre" (*Endless* 211). His 1957 poem "Tentative Description of a Dinner to Promote the Impeachment of President Eisenhower" gives early voice to the growing movement warning of the impending diasaster to the ecological chain of being, an issue which has continued to claim Ferlinghetti's attention:

> And after it became obvious that the strange rain would never stop and that Old Soldiers never drown and that roses in the rain had forgotten the word for bloom and that perverted pollen blown on sunless seas was eaten by irradiated fish who spawned up cloud leaf streams and fell onto our dinnerplates.
>
> (*Starting* 41)

In the very next strophe, he identifies by juxtaposition the way of thinking which he believes to be the source of the projected catastrophe:

> And after it became obvious that the President was doing everything in his power to make the world safe for nationalism his brilliant military mind never having realized that nationalism itself was the idiotic superstition which would blow up the world.

The indictment is a recurrent one in Ferlinghetti's prose and poetry. "As a civil libertarian with anarchist sympathies" (*Seven Days*), he condemns nationalism as an obsolete form of government and the source of petty rivalries which explode into intolerable wars. He asks poignantly, " . . . who wants Nation, and what good is Nation and Nationalism per se, a medieval form of vestigial barbarism to be cast off in all its forms . . ." ("Genesis" 446). He projects a world with "all national flags made into snotrags" (*Mexican* 9) and, in "The Situation in the West followed by a Holy Proposal," celebrates the proposed result: "blessed be the fucking world with no more nations" (*Starting* 64).[2] The coarseness of the image and the toughness of the language underline the strength of his feelings. However, discovering a viable option remains a continuing problem. Ferlinghetti addresses the alternative vaguely:

> The whole world has got to be run by a huge supranational non-political central planning agency.
>   It's got to be a form of humanitarian socialism: not authoritarian, but a nontotalitarian socialism. I'd like to think it could be a kind of Buddhist socialism.
>
> (Meltzer 146)

After the abolition of nations, however that may be accomplished, he suggests that "supra-national law from then on shall concern itself only with the maintenance of eternal peace and ecological balance in the universe" (*Artist's Diatribe*), goals toward which one can scarcely imagine dissent. If the proposal remains idealistic, Ferlinghetti's primary objection to nationalism nevertheless emerges clearly: authoritarian power of any sort is anathema. An idealized individuality results in his 1983 assertion that in a post-national program

> the basic principles of philosophical anarchism—which holds that man is not inherently evil (contrary to what Christians believe) and is capable of voluntarily governing himself for the greater good of the community—shall be allowed to see if they really work.
>
> (*Artist's Diatribe*)

An early poem illustrates the extent of his assertion of individuality and independence. In "Not like Dante," he rejects the Italian poet's vision of Paradise, which Ferlinghetti contemns as

"the perfect picture of / a monarchy"; he instead envisions a
heaven where

> ... there would be no fires burning
> in the hellish holes below
> in which I might have stepped
> nor any altars in the sky except
>   fountains of imagination.
> (*Coney* 28)

He rejects, even in heaven, the notion of a controlling power
governing by means of threats of punishment and demands of
service.

Ferlinghetti's criticism of capitalism pursues two basic directions; the mindless exhaustion of natural resources and the
social and economic inequities. He points out, "Capitalism is an
outrageously *extravagant* form of existence which is leading to
an enormous ecological debacle unless it is completely changed"
(Meltzer 145). As might be expected, the poetic treatment of the
wastefulness of capitalism, of what he characterizes as "the
dominant material mechanical militarist Mammon money
America" ("Genesis" 447), is essentially polemical, suffering far
too often from the preachy didacticism already noted. Thus, for
example, in "Autobiography" his point is overt:

> I have read the Reader's Digest
> from cover to cover
> and noted the close identification
> of the United States and the Promised Land
> where every coin is marked
> In God We Trust
> but the dollar bills do not have it
> being gods unto themselves. (*Coney* 63)

Much more successful is his portrayal of the inequities inevitably accompanying capitalism, primarily because he establishes
his point in a dramatically effective fashion. In "The Billboard
Painters," two pale workers paint a luscious "paradise on earth"
of a sunburned couple enjoying a South Seas island tropical vaca-
tion, a visionary ideal available to the workers only in imagination. However, the narrator encounters the sign only midway
through completion, " . . . as if / the other half of the world had /
still to be provided for" (*Landscapes* 29). In "Two Scavengers in
a Truck, Two Beautiful People in a Mercedes," Ferlinghetti cap-

tures a brief graphic moment of juxtaposition between the four
characters of the title, illustrating " . . . that great gulf / in the
high seas / of this democracy" (*Landscapes* 27). In a much earlier
poem, Ferlinghetti creates a parable to indicate his disappointment at the failure of the democratic system. In "Sailing thru
the straits of Demos," a location whose eagles, elephants, and
donkeys clearly represent the American government, the narrator must (in a passage derived from Pound's first Canto) "so
set forth once more," arriving at the suburbs "of that great
American / demi-democracy."   There, rediscovering Homeric
frontiers in a variation of Keats's "On First Looking into Chapman's Homer," the narrator and his fellow sojourners

>   looked at each other
>   with a mild surprise
>   silent upon a peak
>   in Darien. (*Coney* 12)

"In a Time of Revolution for Instance" (*Open* 10-12) offers
another epiphanic dramatization of the chasm between classes.
Three "very beautiful" people, two of them men and the third a
young woman, enter a café where the narrator has just ordered
lunch. He imagines them ordering something exotic, whereas
elsewhere in the café "a lot of little people sat / quietly eating
their quite ordinary / lunches," including the narrator whose
"fish finally arrived looking / not quite unfrozen and / quite
plastic," making him feel like the classic film image of the little
guy, "like Charlie Chaplin eating his shoe." Enchanted by an
unobtainable dream, the narrator comes to a realization which
Ferlinghetti emphasizes through italics: "I could not imagine
her *carrying* / a carbine."[3] Finally, the narrator concludes with a
revealing projection of a society in which class distinctions have
been eliminated, again employing typographical emphasis to
highlight his point: "under other circumstances / *in a time of
revolution for instance* / she might have fucked me." Typically,
sex is a major process and product in Ferlinghetti's view of a
transformed social order, as though endorsing the Marquis de
Sade's statement in Peter Weiss's *Marat / Sade*: "And what's the
point of a revolution / without general copulation" (130).
      An interweaving Lawrentian celebration of sex, sun, and
art characterizes Ferlinghetti's idealized society. Asked in a 1965
interview, "What do you think the role of the poet should be in
times such as we are witnessing today?" he replied, "Fuck for

peace" (*Idiot* 16). Similarly, the "holy proposal" of "The Situation in the West followed by a Holy Proposal" is that "to fuck is to love again" (*Starting* 62), and Ferlinghetti recommends international copulation to relieve the Cold War: "And blessed be the fruit of transcopulation / and blessed be the fruit of trans-population / and blessed be the fucking world with no more nations" (*Starting* 64). To those who might object that such a solution is unrealistic, especially on an overpopulated planet, Ferlinghetti offers his poem "Overpopulation," which concludes with a "purple blond" who accosts and seduces the narrator, who comments, "None of us will ever die / as long as this goes on" (*Starting* 32). A passage from "The Situation in the West . . . " serves virtually as a prosaic gloss on the earlier "Overpopulation": "And never mind the overpopulation / Contraception can contain / all but love" (*Starting* 64). To be sure, this program of emancipation through copulation may often resemble the allegedly adolescent naiveté of the 1960s hippies and flower children, and Ferlinghetti even endorses this connection:

> I had a poem called *After the Cries of the Birds Have* [sic] *Stopped* — it saw the world of the future where all that was left were roving bands of mystics . . . like those that we call mutants today would be the only ones left. Roving bands of long-haired mystics . . . the whole materialistic ideal of Western man in his business suit would go down the tube. (Meltzer 146)

However, Ferlinghetti's imagery and language suggest his awareness of the practical limitations of this projection. A passage from "Sunrise, Bolinas" seems designed to temper the idealistic visions of "After the Cries of the Birds":

> Such presumption, such perversity
> to mistake bird-cries for song
> when they may really be
> cries of despair.
> (*Open* 27)

Furthermore, Ferlinghetti recognized early the impossibility of his dreams:

> and I am perpetually waiting
> for the fleeing lovers on the Grecian Urn
> to catch each other up at last
> and embrace. ("I Am Waiting," *Coney* 53)

The lovers on the urn never will embrace. Of course, recognizing one's goals as unattainable does not deny the beauty or the value of those ideals. More damaging then is the apparent recognition that the life of sexual sensation has natural physical limitations: "And then the endless attempts to escape . . . the bald hills of burned out sensation" ("Endless Life," *Endless* 211) —a Sibyl of Cumae realization that one's life span may extend beyond the ability to appreciate the pleasures identified as life's values. Ferlinghetti also recognizes that a sexual revolution implies a system of dynamics in which individual roles are treacherous and vulnerable. The variant conclusions' of "In a Time of Revolution For Instance" bear eloquent testimony to this awareness. The alternatives, in order of published appearance, are as follows:

> *in a time of revolution for instance*
> I *could* have fucked her (*New Directions* 23, 46);

> in a time of revolution for instance
> I *could* have fucked her (*Lemming* 4);

> *in a time of revolution for instance*
> she might have fucked me (*Open* 12);

> *in a time of revolution for instance*
> we might have made it. (*Endless* 102)

Here, by means of a series of changes in language and emphasis, the author considers the problems of whether the process of revolution or its resultant sexual emancipation is more important, of the aggressive and ambiguous connotations of the word "fuck," of the possible charges of sexism. The final version, evidently considered most satisfactory by the poet, is both a retreat and an advance. While it steers away from an overt statement of sexuality, opting instead for the implications of a euphemistic expression, it now embraces a creative connotation in which both characters of the clause's subject are assumedly willing and equal participants.

The sun serves Ferlinghetti as a symbol of regenerative light and human consciousness. In "The Man Who Rode Away," which is dedicated to D. H. Lawrence, he recognizes the earlier writer's celebration of that symbol: "Dead Lawrence . . . locked away from the light / of your dead sun" (*Open* 34).

Throughout his poetry, Ferlinghetti uses the sun conventionally as a symbol of life and light. In addition, he uses it to represent the human mind. In his earliest published interview, Ferlinghetti was asked, "Who or what is God?" The poet's answer was brief: "Consciousness" (Mezzetta 3). In *Tyrannus Nix?* he emphatically reiterates the belief that "the only god of life on earth is consciousness itself" (22). The connection between the sun and this consciousness is established and developed in "Letter to a Young Poet in Cuba or Maybe Spain," which concludes,

> But the mind is still the sun
> traveling through the sky
> And the mind also rises
> Abrazos revolucionarios
> mis hermanos del Sur. (*Open* 86)

The rising mind and sun here parallel the uprising of revolutionary spirit. Similarly, "The Situation in the West . . . " concludes with the image of the sun in a revolutionary world:

> we'll all still have the sun
> in which to recognize ourselves at last across the world
> over the obscene boundaries. (*Starting* 64)

In "Insurgent Mexico," the congruence is underlined by the pun on the word "revolution," both as the turning of the earth on its axis and as insurgency:

> In scorched dry desert
>   where sun is god and god eats life
> great god sun going down
>   pastes up immense red posters
>   on adobe walls
> and then falls down
>   over the horizons
>   'with the flare of a furnace blast'
> and the posters faded yellow
>   fall into darkness
>   leaving only shadows to prove
>   one more revolution has passed.
>   (*Who* 54)

A similar pun, this time on the word "reflection," controls another poem, "Upon Reflection," in which

> Daytime moon
> after much reflection says
>   Sun is God. (*Who* 46)

Ferlinghetti also explores the literary backgrounds of the sun symbol, particularly in allusions to the opening stanza of "The Rubáiyát of Omar Khayyám" with its description of the wakening of day:

> The sun the sun behold the sun
> Great God Sun still riseth
> in our rubaiyat
> and strikes the towers with a shaft of light
>   ("The Situation in the West . . . ," *Starting* 61);
>   Yes wake o wake
>   for the sun that riseth
>   with the rising wind
>   will all too soon
>   o all too soon
> our turning world consume (*Back*);
>   Sun Sun
>   Ah sun Om sun
>   Sun Sun Sun
>   Great God Sun
>   Still riseth in our Rubaiyat
>   and strikes and strikes
>   And strikes the towers
>   with a shaft of light!
>   ("Big Sur Sun Sutra," *Open* 120)

Clearly, the light which the sun delivers is aligned with artistic illumination, as Ferlinghetti makes manifest in "Night Light":

> Yet sun bursts forth upon the land
> And a butterfly lights in it
>   upon my hand
> And lights these songs
> and lights these songs
>   in air. (*Open* 124)

This poem embodies its own message: after a focus on night, death, blackness, despair, and age, the poem suddenly shifts in this last stanza to the qualities of art which allow humanity to climb above the world's bleakness into a golden realm of illuminated—and illuminating—song.

As an artist, Ferlinghetti feels an especial commitment to oppose the authoritarian forces of repression which threaten to cast innocence as "people with roses / behind the barricades" ("Assassination Raga," *Secret* 7). He has been repeatedly outspoken about his objections to American poets and small presses accepting government grants, explaining,

> *The State, whether capitalist or Communist, has an enormous capacity to ingest its most dissident elements.*
> . . . You do have the choice of deciding whether or not you are ingested by the state voluntarily and thus becoming a functioning part of it—nourishing it symbiotically, so to speak. The carrot and the stick—*Waiting for Godot* still—Pozzo with Lucky the artist on a string—. (Meltzer 138-39)

This idea is presented poetically in "Dissidents, Big Sur," where the defiant crows caw their objection to the intrusion of an automobile; finally,

> the crows now too
>   wing away on wind
>   and are sucked up
>   and disappear
>   into the omniverous [sic] universe
> Even as any civilization
>   ingests its own most dissident elements. (*Who* 41)

Though the analogy does not work very precisely, the image remains powerful. However, the role of the artist, particularly if he has no specific, practical program to alleviate social problems and if he has little faith in the corrective powers of artistic dissent, is a confusing one. However, as George Steiner points out, the artist must persist despite the discouragement of possible, or even probable futility:

> The informing context of personal creation is always social and collective. Responsibilities and needs are shared. The writer owes lucidity to his society, even if this lucidity seems powerless to effect short-range political ameliorations. (36)

Ferlinghetti admits,

> i'm a relay runner
> with a hollow baton
> with a screwy message in it

> which i can't quite decipher
> a strange message
> an ecstatic message.
>   ("Big Fat Hairy Vision of Evil," *Starting* 16-17)

The poet then becomes another runner in the ages-old artistic relay race toward human happiness. The words "ecstasy" and "ecstatic" (and "mystery" in more recent works) recur throughout the volumes of Ferlinghetti's poetry, for the "ecstatic message" is the song itself,

> some dharma
>   whose name I could
> conceivably sing
>   yet cannot yet decipher.
>   ("Through the Looking Glass," *Secret* 30)

Threatened with annihilation, humanity must seek its salvation in the unknowable but thrilling mysteries of art and love. Ferlinghetti suggests that the "bird of life" which "makes as if to devour us"

> cannot do it
> as long as we keep singing
>   and making love.
>   ("*Voix Glauque*," *Over All* 30)

The artist's role is critical, for he "bears Eros" ("He with the Beating Wings," *Over All* 33), thus satisfying both needs. Thus, watching the coverage of Robert Kennedy's funeral on television, he turns off the sound and plays a raga on his stereo. Confronted by images of death and violence, he recognizes that the

> sitar sings its only answer
> sitar sounds the only sound
> that still can still all violence
> ....
> There is no god but Life
> Sitar says it Sitar sounds it
> Sitar sounds on us to love love & hate hate.
>   ("Assassination Raga," *Secret* 9)

The music of art then provides the heathy impulse toward life and love, a goal which Ferlinghetti feels is being ignored:

> . . . the American painter [has] become increasingly provincial, increasingly isolated in his know-nothing-but-art, do-nothing-but-art attitudes and life-style.
>
> Painting, sculpture and architecture today suffer together from having no dynamic original ideas for the interpretation of life, no live ideas or novel insights for the subjective interpretation of observed phenomena, no articulated scheme—esthetic, social or political—for the overall interpretation of the world today.
>
> (*Artist's Diatribe*)

Riding a bus through wintry Moscow, Ferlinghetti suddenly hears Segovia playing on the radio, and "Segovia comes on / like the pulse of life itself." Asked "What is important in life?" "Segovia says Nada but keeps on playing / his Answer" ("Moscow in the Wilderness, Segovia in the Snow," *Secret* 40-48). Ferlinghetti's vision of art's value lies precisely in that "pulse of life," in an energetic vitality, a determined crusade for the life principle, and an assertion of universal freedom. His poetry continually illustrates his belief that "the fate of the world / depends upon / the way we live" ("Las Vegas Tilt," *Open* 108).

Notes

[1]("Exploits" 193). Ferlinghetti's familiarity with this Jarry work seems clear: the monkey figure in *Ha-Ha* (*Routines* 29-31) appears to be directly derived from Jarry's novel, specifically Chapter 10, "Concerning the Dogfaced Baboon Bosse-de-Nage, Who Knew No Human Words But 'Ha Ha'" (196-98).

[2]After delivering an unwelcome "diatribe on nationalism in general" in Nicaragua, Ferlinghetti tempers his criticism of nationalism in this case:

> A young nation just struggling free of centuries of colonialism, Sandinist Nicaragua sees nationalism as the way to independence. Carlos Fuentes said, "Mexico found that it had to be a nation before it could be a democracy." . . . perhaps Central America must be one nation before it can be a democracy—a new nation (conceived in liberty, etc.) whose states will be safe from being picked off one by one by foreign powers or ideologies—in effect preventing that very "domino" action which U. S. foreign policy has used to justify its overt covert war on Communism in Central America. (*Seven Days*)

[3]Earlier printings of this poem in *Lemming* and *New Directions in Prose and Poetry 23* broadened the typographical emphasis by underscoring or italicizing the entire clause.

Toward a "Third Stream Theatre"

Lawrence Ferlinghetti was one of the early practitioners of the "new theatre," and his two volumes of plays, *Unfair Arguments with Existence* and *Routines*, explore the dimensions and strategies of dramatic innovation. The influence of Bertolt Brecht, Jean Genet, Antonin Artaud, Samuel Beckett, and Eugène Ionesco can be easily detected in many of his productions as he experiments with the forms and structures of drama. Ferlinghetti uses the expressive power of noise and silence, the disintegration of language, the integrity of production autonomy, and the involvement of the audience to disturb the conventional ambiance of the theatre, replacing the traditional with what he calls "Third Stream Theatre." Eschewing the professionalism and virtuosity of his acknowledged influences, Ferlinghetti provides effective and significant contributions to experimental theatre. His avant-garde techniques and structures are employed in the service of a restrained optimism which, in the face of dehumanizing forces, proffers the possible solutions of underground retreat and rebellion, ultimately endorsing the flawed but crucial ideal of selfless love.

In 1966, Robert Brustein called for a "third theatre," offering "artistic license" as an alternative to serious dramas and those with commercial appeal (8). Two years earlier, Ferlinghetti had defined his own dramatic form as

> a "third stream" between oldstyle dramas & spontaneous Action or improvisation, between Well Made Plays (with their coherent pictures of coherent worlds which now turn out to be the falsest) and those free-form Happenings made of primitive perceptual chaos. . . .
> (*Routines* 2)

Ferlinghetti's plays in *Unfair Arguments with Existence* lean more toward the "oldstyle dramas" and his *Routines* more toward the fledgling Happenings, but in both cases the author takes considerable liberties with the model forms. Ferlinghetti characterizes his "routines" as "nexuses of ordinary dramatics, nubs of normal plays" (*Routines* 1-2), and at first glance many of the routines do seem to have been printed in the seed stage. They are essentially situations, episodes, notions, and momentary insights, whose distortion and lack of development give them the quality of political cartoons. Most of the plays in *Routines* disdain dialogue, relying instead on elemental auditory or visual effects. Non-verbal cries and screams and surrealistic images, such as a woman's head carried on a stick or a naked woman whose body is painted to resemble a bearded lady, dominate these plays.[1] Low humor, farce, and slapstick are also employed to enhance the alogical pattern, with mixed results. Occasionally, these devices remain prankish and adolescent. Thus, in *The Victims of Amnesia*, the fact that the Night Clerk repeatedly "*picks nose, eats it*" (*Unfair* 43), together with his Army drill practice in the lobby of the hotel, seems to constitute the limits of Ferlinghetti's efforts at characterization in this instance (the similarity to the discoveries in the peeping Tom scene of John Barth's *The End of the Road* makes Ferlinghetti's use especially unfortunate). The Schmuck of *Motherlode* (*Unfair* 57-76) marks his entrance in Three Stooges fashion by kicking the Miner in the back and clouting him with a rolled magazine. Near the beginning of this play, the Miner struggles to get his mule to move by lifting each of its legs consecutively. A photographer in the same play follows a routine wherein he sets up a cardboard nude and rushes to his camera, whereupon the nude falls over; he rushes back, stands it up, etc. However, similar devices with delicate portrayal or timely use of action and inaction can produce affecting results. In *The Alligation*, Shooky enacts the theme of frustration which characterizes all of the plays: he raises himself to look out the window, then "*Falls to floor, half raises self to window again, falls again, moves to another window, raises self slowly, falls back, half raises self again, falls back, half raises self again, falls back*" (*Unfair* 22). However, Ferlinghetti, unable to resist the appeal of a bizarre and ribald sexual joke, mars a moving, if only partially successful, dramatic polemic by the conclusion, in which Shooky sexually attacks Ladybird, reducing the play from the level of a significantly humane statement to sophomoric bawdry.[2]

Because the possibility of effective oral communication is no more feasible as purposeful action than Shooky's attempt to raise himself, dialogue is shunned in the plays, which, when they employ articulation at all, offer only sequential assertions, not interactive commentary. In the longest play in *Routines*, *Servants of the People*, four loudspeakers are mounted on podiums before an audience composed of actors and the general public, and these loudspeakers dominate the play, providing as much meaningful interchange as the separate channels of a radio. The play focuses on the breakdown of communication, beginning with an introductory mingling of various voices in the audience, yielding a fragmented and colliding effect much like the cut-up and fold-in techniques employed by William S. Burroughs; in fact, Ferlinghetti invoked Burroughs's methods in his introductory notes on the plays by his reference to "cut-ups of existence" (1), and *Servants of the People* provides an epigraph from Burroughs ("Swept with con the millions stood under the signs"), which is later in the text folded into a variation on the opening line of Allen Ginsberg's most famous poem, "Howl": "I have seen the best minds of my generation swept with con" (42). When the loudspeakers take over, their language is "*garbled*," filled with empty political babblings and chauvinistic jargon. A woman in the audience is attacked by a perversion of communication, the logical fallacy known as the complex question: she is asked by a loudspeaker, "Have you ever been a member of the Communist Party, when did you join the Communist Party, and when did you finally irrevocably disassociate yourself from the Communist Party?" (47). As the loudspeakers continue, a graduate student rises to confront the mindless politics, but he is shouted down by the audience, and the loudspeakers once again gain control. However, the dissenter evidently has had an effect, because the audience gradually becomes a "*Hum of confused voices*" (49). The loudspeakers merge into a meaningless babble, and finally the controlling fascist forces reveal themselves, drowning out everything with their roars, whistles, and sirens. Typically, inarticulate and non-human sounds dominate Ferlinghetti's plays. In *His Head*, a man's reminiscences about his early love experiences are bombarded by incomprehensible responses: "a headless wailing in the distance" (*Routines* 13), a boy's lispings and cries, and a recording of a woman singing until the "phono goes lower & slower & the singing becomes a croak. It stops with a final long groan" (15). *The Jig Is Up* (*Routines* 21-22) substitutes for human speech screaming, roaring, wailing, and the voice of a truck—its horn, its motor starting, idling, gunned, and roaring off. *Ha-Ha* (*Routines* 29-31) employs a "Laughing Record," fox-trots, explosions, martial music, jazz, and a large monkey who marks his several appearances by saying "Ha-Ha." *An Evening at the Carnival* (*Routines* 32-33) concludes with a battle between *mariachi* music and the *Internationale*. The total effect of these sounds resembles the *Bruitisme*, or "noise music," proposed by the Italian futurist Russolo. At an extreme, the noises can even be brutally humanized: at the end of *Three Thousand Red Ants*, "*The alarm begins to ring. First it whispers, then it shouts*" (*Unfair* 18).

Several of the plays are more dependent on language, but nevertheless subvert this element. The Miner's monologues in *Motherlode* are filled with half-finished phrases and truncated idiomatic expressions. Characters in this play seem completely unaware of one another's vocal expressions, and ironically the Miner wears a hearing-aid; at the end of the second scene, the Miner and the Schmuck deliver their monologues simultaneously, further underlining the frustration of communication. The situation is summed up in *The Soldiers of No Country*: "Only nobody's listening, we're just talking to ourselves, or if they're listening, they can't hear you, or if they do—if they do hear you, don't understand you, miscomprehend you, misunderstand you" (1st *Unfair* 9).[3] Ferlinghetti continually employs verbal sabotage to highlight the communication impasse. Puns are a frequent tool for him. The development of *Sleeper* (*Routines* 18-20) seems to depend largely on the fact that etymologically "jazz" and "jism" stem from the same root. When one recognizes that *The Jig Is Up* centers on the conflict of races in America, the puns in the title become obvious. In *Our Little Trip*, a man who was completely wrapped in a bandage sings, "Oh we are wounded, wound, unwound!" (*Routines* 8). A boy in *His Head* lisps in the ear of a blindfolded man, who replies, "Oh, I see, I see" (*Routines* 13). In *Bearded Lady "Dies"* (*Routines* 34-35), an artist who exhibits paintings allegedly painted anonymously is dubbed "Anonymous Bosch." *The Customs Collector in Baggy Pants* (*Unfair* 77-85) is a collection of ribald jokes and double-entendres, as corny and clichéd as the jokes on vulgar cocktail napkins. In each play, the integrity of language is undermined as words slip and slide around in their meanings, usage, and connotations. Even language about language is sabotaged: the Miner in *Motherlode*, whose pack mule loaded with books and an upright typewriter suggests that he is a symbol of the writer, says, "The Greeks had a—" and never finishes the phrase (*Unfair* 60). No doubt the word the Greeks had for it was *aphasia*. When language is used in these plays, it is groping or disintegrating, in either case a precarious tool for communication.

Because the role of language is reduced in the plays, the dramatic structure has to be refashioned into a more efficient vehicle. In his introductory notes to *Unfair Arguments with Existence*, Ferlinghetti modestly calls his dramas "rough drafts of plays for a new theatre, or for one that barely exists" (vii). The description seems much more appropriate to the scene-like quality of *Routines*, but Ferlinghetti is probably referring to the rough-hewn aspects of many of his plays. As author, he deliberately blurs the outlines of his productions. Characterization is reduced to a miminum, without a concern for personality or character traits. The personae of Ferlinghetti's plays are masks or empty shells of human beings. The playwright recognizes the dangers inherent in plays with such thin character development: "With the strangest problem still how to get real depth of emotion into such visually exciting & seemingly superficial scenes" (*Routines* 3). His rationale seems to stem from a belief that conventional characterization is invalid because identity itself is superficial. Thus, in *Three Thousand Red Ants*, Fat comments, "Make up our identities as we go along, on demand, as needed. Improvised names and faces! Improvised characters!" (*Unfair* 5). As a result, Ferlinghetti's characters are generic, seldom having names, usually referred to in blandly descriptive or occupational terms: Question Man, Blindfolded Man, Watch Salesman, American Diplomat, Graduate Student, etc.[4] In *Three Thousand Red Ants*, the names of the characters, "Fat" and "Moth," are simply abbreviated forms of the generally descriptive terms "Father" and "Mother." The villainess of *The Alligation* is named "Ladybird," but it is instructive to recall Ferlinghetti's disclaimer regarding the use of Eisenhower in his poem "Tentative Description of a Dinner to Promote the Impeachment of President Eisenhower":

> Well, I hope all these people see that the poem is not aimed at Mister Eisenhower personally but at The President. He is a Real

> Nice Man. Just like Dad. Trueblue. Just not too bright in his President's uniform. It's just like the real nice man inside the cop's costume—you may hate the uniform for the power of the state it represents, but the man inside is not *it*. He's just a deluded walking symbol of it.[5]

Ferlinghetti's plays attack not personalities, but the abuse of social roles, and the representatives of those social roles become the personae of his plays.

Ferlinghetti also steadfastly refuses to dictate the elements of production for the plays. By ignoring realism or conventional authenticity, his dramas gain an autonomy which leaves them open-ended. Thus, in *An Evening at the Carnival*, during a battle between *mariachi* music and the *Internationale*, Ferlinghetti concludes: "This goes on indefinitely. Perhaps the native music will sound again & *Fidelista* rise again. No one knows how it will end" (*Routines* 33). Similarly, Ferlinghetti explains, "*The Alligation* can be taken literally in several ways, depending upon the identity of Shooky. He may also be 'represented' as a Man in a Union Suit; his skin may change color; his suit may be striped. Directors should follow their Sisyphitic Noses" (*Unfair* vii).[6] In *Swinger*, Ferlinghetti comments about the major character: "Perhaps she was not naked when she entered but has disrobed in the dance" (*Routines* 16). An introductory note to *The Victims of Amnesia* states: "The female parts may or may not all be played by the same person" (*Unfair* 38).[7] Finally, *BORE* (*Routines* 50-52) presents an impassioned and eloquent manifesto for a revolutionary theatre (resembling in its principles the guerilla theatre of the Yippies) designed to point out and eventually correct the deficiencies of modern society, and the dramatic example which Ferlinghetti appends is tentative and sketchy, protecting the possibility of spontaneity.[8] The performances, thus, have a looseness which allows them to incorporate fresh materials and to adapt themselves to current events. The structure resembles the technique of minstrel poets who altered their materials to affect specific audiences in particular locales. Ferlinghetti pursued this tradition in his "Oral Messages" in *A Coney Island of the Mind*, where the printed form of the poems is not followed word for word in the poet's recording of them (*Poetry Readings*). He used the same device in his poem "One Thousand Fearful Words for Fidel Castro" (*Starting* 48-52): "The poem has less than its thousand words. Ferlinghetti left space for a different ending, in the chance that there could be a change in the political climate" (Charters 83).[9] Likewise, recent editions of *Tyrannus Nix?* offer a coverleaf for the paperbound volume, appending verses entitled "Watergate Rap 1969-1973," absorbing the scandal which surfaced after the original publication of the book. The result is a freedom from restriction and from discipline. The poems and plays become plastic and can be refashioned for the occasion. In *The Victims of Amnesia*, Ferlinghetti speaks directly to the thematic effects of this freedom when the night clerk exclaims:

> I've had enough of this big con game, hear? Get somebody else to ferret things out, get somebody else to get the facts for the Register. I won't put up with it any longer, and I don't have to, either, hear? Make up your own vital statistics! Your own little reasons and rationalizations and aliases and alibis for living! (*Unfair* 54)

Ferlinghetti envisions his plays as "groping toward some tentative mystique" (*Unfair* vii), rather than imposing a vapid or unrealistic panacea. Thus, the autonomy of the dramatic productions ideally provides liberation for the audience as they pursue their own healthy and purposeful lives.

The interaction between performers and audience was addressed in one of the most influential principles espoused by Antonin Artaud in *The Theater and its Double*:

> It is in order to attack the spectator's sensibility on all sides that we advocate a revolving spectacle which, instead of making the stage and auditorium two closed worlds, without possible communication, spreads its visual and sonorous outbursts over the entire mass of the spectators. (86)

Ferlinghetti uses a number of different techniques to break down the conventional barrier between the stage and the audience. The spectators in *Servants of the People* merge with the performers until "it is impossible to tell the real actors from the rest of the audience" (*Routines* 36). In *Our Little Trip*, "The general public, the audience, or all those who come to 'bear witness' to this moment of life are given blankets as they arrive & asked to lie down under them." Clearly, Ferlinghetti's purpose is to destroy the ordinary comfort of the audience at a theatrical performance: he comments, "Naturally they stir restlessly" (*Routines* 5), thus both describing and predicting their behavior. The audience involvement in *The Center for Death* occurs in the middle of the play, as "From time to time the Watch Salesman steps down into the audience & hauls someone into the procession, or tries to, crying 'Time! Time!'" (*Routines* 24).   At times, the performances can become confrontations between the stage and the audience as though they were antagonists.   Thus, in *The Victims of Amnesia*, the night clerk swings a rifle around "*until it is aimed at front row of audience*" (*Unfair* 44), and later "*shakes fist at feet passing at windows, then at audience*" (53). Again, the point is to disturb the comfortable ambiance of the audience as spectators.   The plays demand that the audience become accomplices in the performance, either by requiring their participation or by antagonizing them into reaction.   Occasionally, Ferlinghetti even tries to alter the theatrical setting and to specify the type of audience.   His notes for *Servants of the People*, for example, suggest: "A stage is not needed.   Any place people assemble will do.   But the more distinguished the location the better.   A large, respectable audience is to be preferred to one made up of poets, artists and their ilk" (*Routines* 36).

In addition, Ferlinghetti uses symbols designed to jar the audience out of comfortable, conventional patterns.   In *The Victims of Amnesia*, a woman gives birth to a series of light bulbs, and Ferlinghetti notes, "*Every attempt must be made to convince the spectators of the literal reality of what is happening, since it does happen & is real*" (*Unfair* 45).   The terrain in *Motherlode* is designed to resemble a human leg, a resemblance Ferlinghetti is at considerable pains to establish (*Unfair* 66-67, 67).   The title character of *The Nose of Sisyphus* attempts to push a globe up a playground slide with his nose (*Routines* 54-56). Michael Kirby has commented on the use of these types of symbols:

> Although they may, like everything else, be interpreted, they are intended to stir the observer on an unconscious, alogical level. These unconscious symbols compare with rational symbols only in their aura of "importance": we are aware of a significance and a "meaning," but our minds cannot discover it through the usual channels.   Logical associations and unambiguous details that would help to establish a rational context are not available.   There is no relevant framework of reason to which impressions may be referred. (20)

The surrealistic images, thus, force an engagement on the part of the audience on levels which are not ordinarily involved. Ferlinghetti also has emphasized the value of non-rational communication: he celebrates "Transition from all this so-necessary dramatic anarchism to pure Poetic Action not necessarily logical or rational but with, at best, that kind of inexpressible inchoate meaning that springs from wild surmises of the imagination" (*Routines* 2). Freed from theatrical conventions, the playwright pursues imaginative truth, rather than the limited statements of reason.

Examination of a single Ferlinghetti play reveals more specifically the function of his techniques in the dramatic medium. In *Three Thousand Red Ants*, several concurrent themes are evident which also characterize many of the other plays and routines: man's virtually voyeuristic approach to the world outside his immediate sphere, woman's role in the resultant state of inaction, and the tyranny of the verbal medium contributing to the same disabling result. The play's bizarre setting is provided as "*A great big bed almost anyplace by the sea*" (*Unfair* 3). When one of the characters wants to get up and leave, a door frame is lowered beside the bed. Later, a window frame is dropped to permit them to look out to sea. The play opens with a man named "Fat" awakening, and with him awakens language:

> Mmm— (*silence*) Mmm— (*silence*) M— (*silence*) M— (*silence*) Mo—
> Mo— (*silence*) Moth— (*Sits up.*) Moth? (*Shakes her.*) Moth?
> (*Lies back.*) Moth? (*Silence*) Moth—er? (*Silence. Closes eyes,*
> *whispers.*) Moth! (*silence*) M— Mother? (3)

Fat is represented as an absent-minded, bumbling, but humane man, more interested in cerebration than copulation.   While reading in bed, he becomes fascinated by an ant which has somehow made its way onto his book.[10] The parable of the ant becomes transparently obvious: Fat watches the ant as it crosses the words "man means," after which it falls off the edge, which reminds Fat of three thousand Red Chinese who fell through a cracked ice block and drowned. Fat's concern is somewhat qualified by the fact that he has only read about this disaster in the newspapers, which necessarily removes him from it as a reality: "those three thousand men in the paper who just got drowned" (7). The dialogue of the play serves to emphasize his distance from the tragedy: his wife asks, "Drowned in the where?" and Fat answers, "In the paper— Three thousand troops in Red China that just got drowned in the floods" (7). Nevertheless, Fat's sympathy seems genuine and sincere and appears to be connected with his desire to get out of bed. However, his wife, Moth, laughs off his social concern. She demands, "Promise you'll not get up when the alarm goes off?" (6). She is frightened of ants and uninterested in the deaths of the three thousand soldiers. The ant and the soldiers are all the same to her: "So— a retired department store credit manager dreams about three thousand red ants in China" (10). Moth is interested only in sex. She reads pornographic books, delights in bawdy jokes and sexual innuendo, recalls a recent sexual dream, and continuously attempts to seduce Fat into engaging in sexual intercourse with her. Fat, however, resists and becomes entranced by a reefed ship he sees through his window: through his binoculars he enthusiastically follows the attempts of the passengers to save themselves. A rescue plane flies overhead, and its shadow crosses the bed, upsetting Moth, who finally kicks away the window and gibes at Fat. Political symbolism seems intended here: the plane is red, white, and blue; as it rushes to offer assistance to the endangered passengers, its black shadow invades the privacy of Fat and Moth in their bedroom. More importantly, however, both characters are limited in their perception of the plane: Fat sees it only as potential deliverance, while Moth sees only its frightening shadow.

Both Fat and Moth are substantially removed from the world outside their "bed." Moth is obsessed with recalling her past with Fat—"all those years." Fat is concerned with the present, but distanced from it: he can perceive it only through the newspapers and his binoculars. He is prevented from becoming involved with events, unable or unwilling to influence even the fate of the ant. Fat's inability to act is partially attributed to the debilitating, castrating influence of Moth: he confronts her, asking, "Why you always want to keep us shut in? Always close the window when I open it! Always close the doors! Why, why, why always shut the world out!" (16-17). Their relationship is imaged by a passage Fat reads aloud from a book: "Like the ant queen, she carries the seed of her long-dead Prince Consort around for years" (9). Later, Moth calls Fat "Prince Consort" and repeats the passage from the book. The accusation regarding women here also informs a number of Ferlinghetti's other presentations. In *The Alligation*, Ladybird refuses to grant Shooky his freedom, preferring to keep him in benevolent captivity. The woman in *Swinger* attempts to capture a bull fiddle pendulum, one of Ferlinghetti's typically phallic symbols. She finally embraces it passionately, but only after she has managed to stop its swinging.

However, a more serious danger addressed in *Three Thousand Red Ants* and in many of Ferlinghetti's other plays is the deterioration of the verbal process. Verbal disintegration threatens the relationship between the characters. Fat gets irritated when Moth calls him "Baby," while Moth is perturbed when Fat makes the sound "erk." At one point, Fat and Moth indulge aloud in reveries, each oblivious to the monologue of the other, lost in their own individual obsessions, speaking in tangents. The situation demonstrates the veracity of the statement made by the Graduate Student in *Servants of the People*: "There is no dialogue. We have no basis for conducting one. And this is the true sadness of our position" (*Routines* 47). In *Three Thousand Red Ants*, speech patterns are continually interrupted and truncated, like the very names of the characters. Puns, language distortions, and verbal associations constantly sidetrack the characters from the active pursuit of their ideas. Verbal dislocation and subversion keep the two characters from the achievement of any purpose, whether sexual or social. The very audience itself is condemned along with the characters. When the window frame is lowered between the bed and the audience, Fat, ostensibly watching those endangered by the reefed ship, shouts encouragement. Moth tries to calm him down, and her words are obviously intended to apply both to the ship's passengers and to the audience: "They can't hear you, way out there" (15). By the end, an egg cup which Fat has broken, a dream he has had of eating an egg on the ice, the broken ice in Red China, a crack in the lens of the binoculars, and a crack he sees in the sky, all merge to image the fragmented psychological state: Fat is, as Moth calls him, a "Humpty Dumpty" (18).

Like many of Ferlinghetti's other plays, *Three Thousand Red Ants* ends at a bleak impasse. Anticipating charges of pessimism, Ferlinghetti has pointed to "the symbolism of light in several plots" (*Unfair* vii). Following the helpful intervention by the rescue plane, the sun appears and sheds radiance. However, the dilemma of the protagonists remains unresolved, and the brightening of the atmosphere seems contrived, at odds with the rest of the play. A more revealing illustration of Ferlinghetti's stance is offered by the conclusion of *Our Little Trip*. In this play, the Question Man badgers a couple: "Will or will not the individual endure, the free ego, the individual identity, will it always somehow manage to reassert itself in spite of all, no matter what it has to go through, no matter what it is subjected to, in spite of all—" (*Routines* 10-11). The focus then shifts to the couple: "The two figures press against each other, fall to the ground and lie together, seeming to caress each other with a low moaning" (11). This scene seems to offer Ferlinghetti's standard optimism in the power of the sensual experience—except that the two figures are completely wrapped in bandages. Though evidently inspired by the Topor drawing which appears on the front cover of *Routines*, their embrace has the chilling quality of the featureless kissing figures in René Magritte's painting *Les amants*. The optimism of the play is muffled, restrained: the proper instinct is there, but it is stifled by the conditions of existence. The tone of Ferlinghetti's plays is one of only wishful or tentative optimism, a condition he sees as integrally interwoven with the theatre itself: "Thus, feeling around on the frontiers of theatre, we may yet possibly discover some 'seeking action' in life itself" (*Unfair* ix). The possibility of this discovery inspired much of the dramatic experimentation of the 1960s and led many of the playwrights to neglect stage polish and sophistication and to focus instead on visionary ideals of regeneration. For Ferlinghetti, dramatic experimentation has a moral purpose: the liberation of the theatre and freedom from dramatic conventions can offer the liberation of the individual identity and the free ego, and the "new theatre" can thus contribute to the evolution of the new human being.

In his introductory notes to *Routines*, Ferlinghetti describes his plays as "liberations (from all the old hang-ups— phenomenological, neurotic, Reichian, literary, theatrical, political), liberating catastrophes . . . " (1). These hang-ups become villainous in his plays because they are dehumanizing and they lock their victims in patterns which afford no escape. Thus, Ferlinghetti portrays the vulnerability of the disadvantaged to the forces of wealth and power in *The Alligation* and defines the title's key word as "any connexion, situation, relationship,

Les amants
1928
René Magritte
Richard S. Zeisler Collection, New York

obsession, habit or other hang-up which is almost impossible to break" (*Unfair* 20).[11] The social complaints in the plays do not focus specifically on contemporary society, but instead attempt to encompass the range of civilization: in *Ha-Ha* a Moloch-like furnace of liberty makes increasing demands of babies from women progressing from ancient Troy through medieval Europe and the American "Roaring Twenties" into a nondescript future. The implication that history's females heartlessly sacrifice their offspring as fodder seems characteristic of Ferlinghetti's criticism of women. In *Three Thousand Red Ants*, Moth attempts to dominate and control, to imprison and confine Fat, just as Ladybird imposes similar limitations on Shooky in *The Alligation*, apparently in both cases as a way of prolonging the illusion of the women's youth, of pretending to disregard the passage of time. Thus, Moth disdains the wrecked ship while examining her face in the mirror of a compact, commenting, "Repair the ravages of—" (*Unfair* 15), unable to bring herself even to utter the feared word, and Ladybird refuses to admit, despite the physical evidence before her, that her "baby," Shooky, has grown up. In addition, if, as Ferlinghetti states, the light in the plays suggests hope, his female characters are denials of that optimism: Fat reads aloud from a book, "There are, in general, only two kinds of ants. There are light-seeking ants and dark-seeking ants—" (*Unfair* 9), in response to which Moth retreats under the covers and closes her eyes; later, when the sun emerges and sheds a bright radiance, she violently shoves away the window; finally, she protests, "I'm 'light-seeking' too!" (17) and again closes her eyes. Ferlinghetti's male characters, searching for their liberation, find themselves also looking for an idealized woman, for a love which will not be incapacitating and debilitating: the Miner in *Motherlode* comments on women, "Feet of clay! They're all the same, all the same—though I keep hoping—" (*Unfair* 62). The plays also criticize artists, in terms similar to the complaints against women. Each of the two characters in *Sleeper* is identified as a lover, and they stage a musical competition between classical and jazz forms. Similarly, in *Non-Objection* (*Routines* 26-28) two painters emerge from baby carriages and study themselves in mirrors before painting; here again Ferlinghetti provides a sense of historical progression as their competition carries them from crude, primitive sketches, through representation, cubism, abstract expressionism, and action painting. The blatant and juvenile egocentricity of the artists allows for the development of approaches and styles but offers to humanity only futility and the ultimate death of art.

Deprived then of meaningful identity and direction by the failure of political society, of interpersonal relations, and of artistic commitment, the human being is reduced to R. Buckminster Fuller's clinically mechanical definition, which Ferlinghetti quotes at length in *Our Little Trip*:

> Man is a self-balancing, 28-jointed adapter-based biped; an electro-chemical reduction plant, integral with segregated stowages of special energy extracts in storage batteries, for subsequent actuation of thousands of hydraulic and pneumatic pumps, with motors attached; 62,000 miles of capillaries; millions of warning signal, railroad and conveyor systems; crushers and cranes (of which the arms are magnificent 23-jointed affairs with self-surfacing and lubricating systems, and a universally distributed telephone system needing no service for 70 years if well managed); the whole, extra-ordinarily complex mechanism guided with exquisite precision from a turret in which are located telescopic and microscopic self-registering and recording range finders, a spectroscope, *et cetera*, the turret control being closely allied with an air conditioning intake-and-exhaust, and a main fuel intake.
>
> Within the few cubic inches housing the turret mechanisms, there is room, also, for two sound-wave and sound-direction-finder recording diaphragms, a filing and instant reference system, and an expertly devised analytical laboratory large enough not only to contain minute records of every last and continual event of up to 70 years' experience, or more, but to extend, by computation and ab-stract fabrication, this experience with relative accuracy into all corners of the observed universe. There is, also, a forecasting and tactical plotting department for the reduction of future possibilities and probabilities to generally successful specific choice. . . .
>
> (*Routines* 7)

In this play Ferlinghetti indites a condemnation of humanity's material obsession, a complaint which glances irreverently off of the opening lines of Wordsworth's "The World Is Too Much with Us": "Getting and spending we lay waste our trousers, and our little trip is rounded with a slip—into eternity—" (5).[12] The paired central figures of the play have their bodies wrapped by the ends of a single bandage, suggesting that a bandage, for common or similar wounds, provides the only connections between human beings in a brutally unfeeling and acquisitive society.

Without meaningful goals or a significant sense of direction, life becomes arbitrary and senseless, as the night clerk in *The Victims of Amnesia* makes manifest: "All of you! With your blind feet! Taking you who knows where! Like as if any of you even knew what brung you in here! Incomprehensible transients! Inscrutable wanderers!" (*Unfair* 53).

However, Ferlinghetti's plays do offer the notion that change can be effected, although his message suggests that this can only be achieved outside of conventional channels. The Miner in *Motherlode* asks rather explicitly, " . . . do you think it's at all possible to find the ideal— the ideal society?" (*Unfair* 63) and later recognizes that, "if you want to get the goods out of this earth, you've really got to dig, my friend, not just scratch the silver service, let me tell you" (64)—that is, to go beneath the service/surface, to go underground. *The Alligation* echoes this belief: "Like the aardvark, the alligator frequently digs himself an underground retreat" (*Unfair* 26). Only by retreating from a coarse world of selfish and commercial interests, tainted by vulgarity, insensitivity, and artificiality, can the writer/Miner hope to avoid contamination of his integrity and to escape the amoeba-like engulfment of his vision. Ferlinghetti seems to have had precisely this issue in mind in his "Translator's Note" to *Selections from Paroles* by Jacques Prévert,[13] where his word choice reflects the same imagery:

> It would seem that the enormous success of PAROLES (several hundred thousand copies in print) went to the wrong part of his head. In his later books, instead of becoming more profound, he allowed his naturally cinematic eye too easy a passage over the still-astounding surface of the world. While below the surface others began digging a world the most omnivorous eye could never reach. (5)

This description of Prévert's vision is especially noteworthy for *Motherlode* in that the Schmuck makes his appearance in the guise of a cinematic producer. Ferlinghetti suggests that a writer's very success as a gadfly of the controlling society can lead to rather seductive celebration and popular success, which can in turn blind him to the societal problems whose delineation propelled the writer to fame. For Ferlinghetti, the writer (and, of course, the citizen) must persist in rebellion against the stifling and debilitating strictures of contemporary life, adopting as his program the manifesto offered in his routine *BORE*:

> dedicated to the creation of "situations" in public places whenever some social, political or cultural event needs to be protested against due to its fatuousness, general stupidity, innocuousness, or whatever else offensive to the open mind & spirit. (*Routines* 51)

However, even the retreat to the underground, away from the spotlights and headlines, becomes an alternative jeopardized by potential disaster. Thus, the Miner celebrates his active withdrawal:

> Dug my own— little— (*Pick comes loose, and he swings again.*) That's it— We dig our own— (*Swings again.*) our own little old— beds— our own— (*breathing hard, trying to pull himself out*) One doesn't— just— sink— into the ground— by— by gravity!
>
> (*Unfair* 75)

The fragmentation of his monologue, coupled with the word choice concluding the passage, indicates that he is also digging his own grave. This would seem to severely qualify any optimism in this option, despite the fact that Ferlinghetti characterizes the play as leaving "the way open to hopeful new gonopoietics" (*Unfair* viii).

"We're all in a gutter," Fat exclaims early in *Three Thousand Red Ants* (*Unfair* 5), but the Oscar Wilde allusion also suggests the hope: Wilde's sentence continues, "but some of us are looking at the stars" (*Lady Windermere's Fan*, Act III). The particular stars Ferlinghetti is looking at are the unselfish tenderness and innocence whose loss is mourned in *The Soldiers of No Country*:

> I gave up the "real" long ago! My mother was an actress, and she was *always* acting. Even when my father died, my mother wept with only one eye. The other she kept clear to see the effect on me, the audience. By the time he died they acted as if there had never been anything between them, as if there'd *never* been any tenderness or any innocence— between them, ever— as if they'd never seen each other at all, all that time— saw only themselves—. (1st *Unfair* 12-13)

Without love's affection, life becomes a regrettable evasion of human contact and interrelation. Ferlinghetti focuses on the same problem in his novel, *Her*:

> Everyone and every body was losing contact. Every body. That was it. Bodies were getting more and more out of contact with each

> other, though they were still used for making love. Making love
> was supposed to be a means of learning about love itself. . . . Making
> love was a means of proving that life existed, a means of proving
> that love itself, spiritual love, was something that existed. (132)

The underground withdrawal becomes a useful vehicle but a
sorry home. The Miner seems driven to his grave-like escape in
a "desert waste" by disappointment and disillusionment, while
the mynah birds flit about crying aloud what he has chosen to
abandon: "*Love! Love!*" and "*live, live*" (*Unfair* 71-76). The
trench the Miner digs becomes an ironic Beckettian womb-tomb.
Ferlinghetti described its attractiveness in *The Soldiers of No
Country*:

> And in dreams we return to where there are no nationalities—
> yes— as in the womb again, for in the womb we are in no country, we
> are the soldiers of no country, the great unborn of no country, and
> lead a blind life of our own, a blind life that knows no evil or hate,
> knows only a blind urge to love, to be born and to love and to love
> and to give birth again—. (1st *Unfair* 19)

However, this "blind urge to love" suggests nothing of willful
human commitment, engagement, the conscious determination
toward love. Ferlinghetti uses the language of the play to highlight the distinction. The Miner, adapting the line from Philip
Lamantia which serves as the play's epigraph, comments while
watching the Schmuck's sexual activity with the Model, "Crotch
which once was a vision of love!" (*Unfair* 71), and, as the next
act opens, he gazes off out of his trench, bordered by "*hair-like
underbrush*" (72), at the distant woods, describing them as
"Crotch in the wood which once was a— a nest, of sorts" (72).
The play concludes with a glance at those woods, pulling together the various imagistic threads: "*The birds, nested now in
crotch of wood, lisp 'Love, love!' very distantly, like an echo of
themselves*" (76). The Miner's retreat may help him evade the
heartbreak of human entanglement, but it also deprives him of
the concomitant development. Nothing grows in this vacuum.
The road of human love and commitment may be gouged by pot-
holes of pain, misunderstanding, and grief, but all persons are
blessed who can conclude with the bandaged woman in *Our
Little Trip*: "Still—still we have come a long way in our search
for ecstasy—" (*Routines* 10).

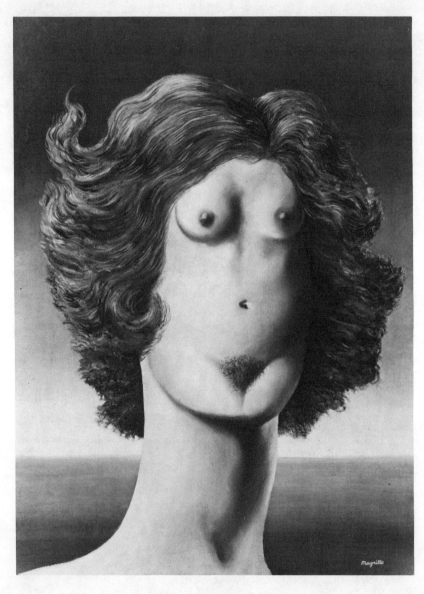

Le viol
1934
René Magritte
Menil Collection, Houston, Texas

Notes

[1]The bearded lady image may have been inspired by the painting *Le viol* by the surrealist René Magritte.

[2]The explicit stage direction was added to printings of the volume after the edition was trimmed from seven to five plays: "*There is a blackout, and strobe lights come on. In their pulsing, Shooky can be seen fucking Ladybird*" (36).

[3]Early printings of *Unfair Arguments with Existence* consisted of seven plays: *The Soldiers of No Country*, the five plays which are retained in later printings, and *The Nose of Sisyphus*. The latter play was incorporated in subsequent printings of *Routines*, and Ferlinghetti has written me that he "suppressed" the former play. Quotations from *The Soldiers of No Country* will be cited in the text by references to the first printing of the volume—(1st *Unfair*).

[4]In possible explanation, Toledano asserts in *The Soldiers of No Country*:

> That's an ancient tribal superstition. If you know someone's name, then you own her—or him. That's why Arabs never say their wives' names in public. They only call them "someone's sister," for instance. (1st *Unfair* 7)

However, the three characters in *The Soldiers of No Country* are all identified by name. By the third printing of the volume *Unfair*, the play includes four named characters.

[5](Jacket notes). The poem appears in *Starting* 41-44.

[6]The latter phrase is an allusion to Ferlinghetti's *The Nose of Sisyphus*, once appearing as the last play in this volume, but later inserted as the final piece in *Routines*.

[7]This introductory note does not appear in early printings of the volume.

[8]A Yippie manifesto is offered by "Free" (pseud. Abbie Hoffman):

> The key to the puzzle lies in theater. We are theater in the streets: total and committed. We aim to involve people and use (unlike other movements locked in ideology) any weapon (prop) we can find. The aim is not to earn the respect, admiration, and love of everybody—it's to get people to do, to participate, whether positively or negatively. All is relevant, only "the play's the thing."
>
> (*Revolution* 27)

[9]The back cover of the original pamphlet publication of the poem contains the following statement:

> There are not one thousand words here. The author has left room for a happier ending, in case the relentless hostility of government and press in the U. S. should somehow not triumph in the end.

[10]In his novel, *Her*, Ferlinghetti refers to "this little lonely ant of consciousness" (128).

[11]This definition does not appear in early printings of the volume.

[12]In his checklist, Kherdian claims that the word *slip* is an error and should be *sleep* (12).

[13]The title of *Our Little Trip* (*Routines* 5-11) may stem from Ferlinghetti's translation "The Conductor" in this volume (*Paroles* 60).

Toward "Underivative Creation"

It was something to do with my mind.
(Brautigan 10)

In his prose volume, *Her*, Lawrence Ferlinghetti explores the dynamics of artistic consciousness and control. He posits as his protagonist Andy Raffine, who is seeking his own unique identity, symbolized by his search for the enigmatic "her" of the title. This quest is frustrated by his reluctant recognition of his role as a fictional character and by his vulnerability to the forces of illusion. In addition, Ferlinghetti allows the relationship between the author and his creation to image a view of the relationship between God and man.

As the narrator of *Her*, Andy Raffine finds himself in the middle of his life, like Dante, in "the wood of the world" (9). Raffine yearns to define his self-consciousness, for he recognizes and calls attention to his role as a fictional construct. The tensions of the novel thus become clear; *Her* focuses on the interrelationship of three figures—the author; a theoretically unique and autonomous literary character; and the hybrid character resulting from the imposition of the author's experiences, fantasies, and language on the "pure" character. Raffine warns the reader, presumably about *Her*:

> Some half-ass poet had invented it all, making up, for square consumption, an imaginary Villon story of lost youth, fabricating romantic goop to fill in the facts nobody knew and which I myself did not remember, adding a narrative voice which was supposed to be myself but was some kind of fourth-person-singular voice I did not recognize.... (23)[1]

In a frenzy of rebellious subjectivity, Raffine interprets everything he encounters in terms of his own identity: "At the stroke of twelve. It was I that was struck, at twelve" (22); "the [house] number I looked for was the same as my age" (27); "the number on his cap was the same as my age" (85). In addition, characters dissolve to become Raffine: "Here a door was my Metro entrance, a blind man by it, with a cardboard box around his neck. . . . He grew younger, fatter, as I watched, became myself . . . " (80). This problem of identity is one which recurs throughout *Her*. The transaction of Andy Raffine with himself is impeded by his own self-awareness, which finds him vacillating between an affected self-effacement and smug self-conceit. At one point, echoing Samuel Beckett's Malone (283), Raffine promises that he "would say I no more," but he continues unchanged, declaring "as I fell between a zero and the infinite I tried to stop myself . . ." (48). Ferlinghetti's approach here closely resembles Alain Robbe-Grillet's description of his own technique:

> Not only is it *a man* who, in my novels for instance, describes everything, but it is the least neutral, the least impartial of men: *always* engaged, on the contrary, in an emotional adventure of the most obsessive kind, to the point of often distorting his vision and of producing imaginings close to delirium. (138)[2]

Raffine is in precisely this delirious stage, occupying a carrefour where reality and illusion intersect and impinge on one another: "In the hushed dark of the park, reality and illusion mixed" (39). A time-leveling aspect, reinforced by the recurrence of specific image patterns and phrases, serves to generalize not only the experience, but also the attitudes and responses. Furthermore, it enables the author to invent rather than to describe these same elements, with the concomitant assumption that this invention is truer than depiction could be. The novel becomes a portrayal of the tension between creative invention and realistic depiction. Raffine returns to situations, redescribing them, trying desperately to ascertain and establish for himself their truth and reality. Manifestations of fantasy and actuality become devices used by Ferlinghetti to explore and delineate a conceptualized reality. Deliberately elongated prose rhythms and hypnotic dream sequences are placed in sharp, contrasting juxtaposition with abruptly banal statements. Cinematic figures of speech also function to emphasize the indeterminacy of chiaroscuro. In addition, *Her* is seeded with images of a static, frozen world, as though actions were caught at a still moment, the time-suspended dream world of a painting or a photograph. As a result, Raffine finds himself rooted, stationary, unable to advance, his world arrested, "suspended in silence" (15). These devices provide for an analytic examination of the nature of subjectivity, which is one of the primary concerns of *Her*. Raffine returns again and again to the same images in order to illustrate the necessity of his quest for self-understanding:

> It was a transaction with myself, and the scene corresponded almost exactly to reality, the negative of it having slipped just a very little while being printed. Like an extra in a grade B movie, I could not walk out of it, trapped in the celluloid sequence. (9-10)

Raffine claims to be "looking for the main character of my life" (10), seeking to assert his own identity through certain touchstones, primarily those of sex and the creative impulse.

Given the complexity of Ferlinghetti's purpose, the reader may often be confused about the identity of the speaker as *Her* progresses. Ferlinghetti confronts such possible response by incorporating the confusion itself into the texture of his work: he allows Raffine to question whether the character's role in the plot and action is one of participant or audience. Because the central issues of *Her* involve artistic creation, many of the arts are called upon to provide imagery illustrating Raffine's uncertainty. He repeatedly finds himself unable to determine whether, to use his own cinematic image, he is an actor playing a role in a movie or simply a member of the audience watching the movie.[3] Indeed, he suspects that he is continually shifting between these positions. Similarly, Raffine suggests that he may be an extra or a member of the audience who wanders onstage and perhaps becomes part of a dramatic production, for "one could not tell the players without a program, for the faces interchanged, fused together" (10). The arts of painting and sculpture also provide appropriate images of identity confusion. Raffine is a painter, but the "her" he seeks is a sculptor. A waiter named Lubin reveals, however, that the girl's statues are, "yes, you guessed it—all herself—all as she imagined her poor sweet self—as she was—as she really was" (69). Raffine had anticipated this notion in an image which highlights the relationship between the artist and his creation: "She was one of her own statues which, failing as stone, had come to life in flesh . . ." (32). Raffine and "her" become artistically entwined as he recognizes that each of the statues in her studio "represented an image in one of my own paintings" (34). Just as Raffine is a character created by Ferlinghetti, "her" is a character created by Raffine.

The artistic images appearing most frequently in *Her* spring from literature.   The language, action, and emphasis of much of the last two sections of the book reflect off a cento passage derived from a prose work by H. D., *Palimpsest*, principally the first story, "Hipparchia: War Rome (*circa* 75 B.C.)," portraying a woman named Hipparchia, who Marius, her lover, feels may be "after all, a creature entirely of his imagining" (28).[4] The very image of a palimpsest is, of course, valuable to the focus in *Her* on how the author writes over his fictional character: Raffine at one point characterizes every human being as "a perambulant palimpsest" (84).   In addition, Ferlinghetti provides numerous allusions to and parodies of familiar passages from famous writers.   The parodies, together with the numerous examples of paranomasia, offer evidence of verbal sabotage. Word associations, Joycean multilingual puns, Dylan Thomas-like word harmonies, and sight and sound puns abound in *Her*, providing continual proof of liberated fancy and the associational capacity of the human imagination.   In many instances, the verbal play adds virtually nothing to the development of the narrative or to the progression of ideas, existing only in a spirit of playfulness and demanding to be taken in this vein.   Raffine sees the verbal medium as one of the chief factors in the creation of illusion and attacks its undermining effect: "words, in their quest for Attic verity, were the real destroyers, the real preventers, each a little fence" (120).   He deprecates "those words and names behind which everyone hid and was hidden and that were the buildingblocks of false identities" (41).   Raffine himself is a victim of verbal imprecision and illusion.   Again and again, he slips inadvertently into falsified apprehension and the pathetic fallacy and finds that he must qualify or correct his perceptions:

> There was a light in a window, a light in a tall window on the first floor of a stone hotel that looked like a temple across the square.   I went toward it, stopped myself halfway, for there I'd gone again straight into old abstractions, seeing that stone building as a temple. It wasn't a temple, it was merely some old hotel (112);

> The [shadows of the] horses had all marched away along the walls, and one of them had left a very small streak of mud along one of her cheeks, or perhaps it was just a leftover shadow, or—no, it was a kind of hoofprint upon her skin, just above where the swelling of her breasts began—no, it was not a footprint, it was a print or a shadow of a very small cross, white against the sur-

rounding skin, as if the sun had—no, there was nothing, all was shadow. (119)

Early in the book, Raffine explains the nature of the problem: "It was a battle with the image, and existence a coiling and recoiling of one's self, with the plot spinning out so smoothly always, although one never could be certain just where one had come in" (10). Thus, the battle is on the field of self between the forces of reality and the forces of illusion.

Her confronts the problem of illusion at another remove: Raffine, who rebels against imagination, is himself a creation of the imagination, trapped in the novelistic venture of the author.[5] The author necessarily contaminates Raffine's transaction by "the old associational turning eye that turns all it sees into its own" (93). The tension that Her portrays is between autonomous self-depiction by the created character and creative invention springing from the author's own experiences. Raffine cries out desperately for autonomous purity, while recognizing his dilemma as "the same creepy nowhere hero making his mushy exiled rounds the same walking cliché never able to break away into the free air of underivative creation" (111). With eminent clarity, he identifies his function as that of a "poupée intérieure" (111) but refuses to surrender to that state. Instead, he struggles against associations, misapprehensions, and stylized behavior. However, in his role as an artist, Raffine encounters the same problems facing his author:

> I had already painted everybody else's painting of the same subject, and I had torn out all the photos in the picture book and scattered them about on the stones of the Square where they lay still looking up at me like so many disheveled characters, and the figures on the terrace were the propped-up portraits of the same subject painted and repainted by different hands before me . . . (14-15);

> —I made one nice clean underivative line, and there it was ready to be made into 'something new,' my brush or pencil poised over it ready to enact the new, but what came, what resulted? The brush came down, lost itself, made the old face, the drippy paint fell back into its old habits, sticking to everything, to the old forms. (112)

Her thus begins to comment on itself and its own creative elements. The illusion of unique creativity is punctured by the

barbs of realistic execution: "the marvelous miraculous painting
. . . the very soul of liberated creation itself, except that I had
trouble with one thing, I still had trouble painting eyes, I had yet
to paint eyes that had the look of undreamy reality in them"
(53)—with Ferlinghetti very likely punning on eye/I. As Robbe-
Grillet has observed:

> The real, the false, and illusion become more or less the subject of
> all modern works; this one, instead of claiming to be a piece of
> reality, is developed as a reflection on reality (or on the dearth of
> reality, as Breton calls it). It no longer seeks to conceal its neces-
> sarily deceptive character by offering itself as a "real-life story."
> (150-51)[6]

In this fashion, the façade of Her as a realistic (or "real-life") story
vanishes before certain admissions: Raffine cites "that endless
bookmovie that some hack had adapted from an endless parade
of figures who might have been myself in a parody of my life
which was itself based upon an endless sexual fantasy centered
on some vague unmet figure of love" (61).

The "sexual fantasy" is inextricably involved with the
ambiguous "her" who encompasses for Raffine both "real" flesh-
ly satisfaction and ideal human fulfillment: "I am on the way to
myself through what I hope is love" (60). He believes "Making
love with bodies was a kind of speech . . . a language of being"
(132). Raffine recounts numerous sexual encounters, ranging
from the innocent of exchanged glances in a cathedral to an
affair with a girl "come to plague to destroy" (140). Woman is
both antagonist and ideal for him, because he realizes that the
phantom figure of "her" is largely a product of his imagination,
"capable of stretching into any form I imagined" (11) and dependent even for action upon his powers: "When I was not looking,
the distant figure would not advance. The sequence arrested,
she stopped dead when I was not looking, yet started off again
simultaneously when my eye fell back on her" (12). "Her"
encompasses all women—mother, the Virgin, Helen, Dante's
Beatrice, Mona Lisa, and Heidi, as well as all those from
encounters in the past, present, and future—with "the various
women I've known all adding up to flash in a composite image
all leading up to this moment in some lost connection with this
Virgin's place" (151). Thus, while Raffine passionately pleads for
his own independent identity, his associational eye deprives the

entire female sex of precisely that uniqueness. To be sure, Raffine admits to a spiritual quest: he is seeking self-discovery, and the enigmatic "her" will be the vehicle for its achievement. However, Raffine's obsession appears to be lust rather than love, flesh rather than spirit, a self-admitted "confusing of sex with love" (154). ". . . I lay, dreaming of breasts and vulvas," he admits (10). Women are seen almost entirely as sexual objects:

> I saw her as a creature entirely alone, her naked body not strange and classic in its unrelievable loneliness, but simply unfinished, incomplete. . . . I had only fully to awaken her, had only to bring her to a new awareness, to an ecstasy she had not yet known. . . . (35)

Raffine claims that he wants to paint a picture depicting

> swimming hordes of women with musk flowers in their hair who waded naked into the sea from their bound, trussed-up shores to climb aboard the great rafts and lash the crew to the decks and masts and climb on top of them and exhaust them in perpetual orgasm, at which point they threw the men fainting into the sea to revive them and then jumped down upon them in the water and rode them coupled in coitus. . . . (55)

This seems more the vision of the misogynous William Burroughs than that of the romantic that Raffine and Ferlinghetti both claim to be. Thus, at one point, Raffine can admit,

> that drone of myself whose organ was contrived by nature only to function in space has now accomplished his admirable ecstasy and falls bleeding to death like an artist who has finally and fatally succeeded in killing the romantic within himself. . . . (110)

Raffine makes a conscious effort to avoid romanticism: "Her hair had a woody smell. I was drunk in the dark of it. Her lips were not illusion, her breasts not white doves" (51). He feels that he cannot idealize woman: "To deify is to betray in a failure of love in some sort of transaction with myself" (147). His vagueness here is characteristic, because it is the "idea of woman" (107) he craves. He rationalizes that sex is a means of asserting the existence of life and love—but this assertion remains only an assumption.

Crucially, Raffine's view of women characterizes them all indistinguishably as incomplete, unfinished, uncommitted, and unawakened. He describes "her" as "an anonymous vessel, an anonymous receptacle into which I could pour myself, pour the history of myself without words, the act of love its own adequate eloquence" (36). His feelings, images, and language correspond to the patterns identified by Catharine R. Stimpson:

> In any situation, men speak a sexual grammar in which women are the subjects of two kinds of sentences: passive, in which they are screwed, taken, burrowed into; or copulative, in which they become vessels, Madonnas, Chicks, or other static complements. (380)[7]

Furthermore, Raffine's phrase "without words" is significant because it calls attention to the parallel between Raffine and his author: Raffine yearns to pour himself into "her," while Ferlinghetti pours himself into *Her*. Both are necessarily frustrated: "Only woman in the abstract retains the possibility of realizing Andy Raffine's ideals" (Ianni 399). Raffine learns that the fulfillment through sexual commingling which he quests is impossible with a merely human partner. The "idea of woman" is purely imaginative. More accurately, it is imagination itself. Raffine is an artist, and his self-discovery must be achieved "through the illusions of sense through the illusions of happiness and beauty" (60). The novel becomes the story of a mind inventing itself. Raffine jumps "into the subway that had turned into a real train" (83), that is, "the train of my thought" (83). "Memory," he tells us, "was the real painter" (114), but the ideal painter is imagination. Raffine's own questionable existence becomes critical at this point, for, obviously, Raffine himself is a fictional construct and can be seen as a vehicle for the artist's attempt to define his situation in the world. Ferlinghetti has explained why his autobiographical attempt must emerge as only "semi-autobiographical": "I was, I am writing my story. . . . But I am not a storyteller . . . since I can't ever find the story, can't tell my story from her-his story, history" (quoted by Serebnick 636). The created characters, he shows, refuse to acquiesce to the author's plan. Once on the stage they begin to ad-lib their own existence.

The original hardbound edition of *Her* included the following epigraph from Camus's *The Rebel*:

> Those who have not insisted, at least once, on the absolute virginity of human beings and of the world, who have not

trembled with longing and impotence at the fact that it is impossible, and have then not been destroyed by trying to love half-
heartedly, perpetually forced back upon their longing for the
absolute, cannot understand the realities of rebellion and its
ravening desire for destruction.

The quest of Raffine, who reluctantly idealizes "the true rebel
hero" (89), for "her" is symbolic of his search for his own
completed self and innocence, figured by the virginal "her" and
the unsullied piece of white string which makes repeated
appearances in the book. Glosses on the significance of the string
appear in Ferlinghetti's poems:

>   . . . she saw the string so white
> so lovely and so beautiful
>   and looking like
>   Innocence itself
> ("with bells for hooves in sounding streets," *Pictures* #19);
>
> And to dream of white string
> a symbol of innocence. ("White on White," *Landscapes* 36)[8]

However, innocence is inevitably betrayed by the mortal conditions of experience, age, and impotence. The possibility of
recaptured purity is ambiguously provided as the recurrent
"flushing of bidets signaled the end of an era" (88), perhaps
slushing away the tainted condition and affording the possibility
of renewal. What Raffine finally craves is synthesis of the
elements of his character, an integration he approximates with a
discovery he eventually makes: "I had lost her anonymous body
in the flow of myself I had absorbed her into my blood and could
not see her any more as the eye could not see itself" (106).
Clearly, the elusive "her" is peripheral to the actual quest.
Raffine, "confusing flesh madonnas with spiritual ones"
(Ferlinghetti quoted on back cover), is seeking more than a
human "her" could provide: "the hero who is always myself
aspires to the absolute" (94). Consequently, he finally recognizes
that "she . . . is not the subject of my story for I myself am the
subject of my sentence and she's the object and I've diagrammed
it all and analyzed the syntax of my sentence in which she's the
object and it's an objective case and she is her in this case which
is the case of myself . . ." (147). The pun on the word "objective"
underscores Raffine's quest for objective perception, for freedom

from associational coloring. Raffine turns from flesh to spirit, from corporeal concerns to ideational ones. Throughout *Her*, he seeks to free himself from his cumbersome body, for he imagines, "only when one of their number freed himself from his clothing of fat flesh that he was able to escape" (37). Flesh represents for him the form of illusion which masks or distorts reality, "the fleshpaint skin I hid in like painters hiding behind their paint, authors behind their words" (134). Liberation from the flesh, then, would parallel liberation from the word, which Raffine can achieve only when freed from the novelist's control, at the conclusion of the novel, "where I'm the noise at the threshold of voiceless silence, where only the fourth person singular remains" (153). In the final section of *Her*, the relationship between the author and his character reveals itself as emblematic of more than literary concern. Religious imagery asserts itself, until finally Raffine exclaims: "who's to know when I wing down into the public domain just what Somebody could have meant by me and what could He possibly have had in mind, as if I were really seriously supposed to be a reflexive pronoun reflecting parastatic Him" (155). Raffine's rebellion thus takes on the dimension of man's revolt against control by his Creator, in Whose likeness he is fashioned. The narrative voice would seem at this point to return to Ferlinghetti himself, rebelling against the chains of humanity and mortality. The rebellion is, of course, fruitless, as hopeless as Raffine's revolt against his author. Reluctantly, Raffine finally adjusts to his literary essence, sheds the fat which earlier had prevented him from passing through the turnstile where the "way had remained open only as long as our thin fictions, we existed only as long as our fictions" (36). He recognizes "this site of myself made into the reassuring form of a story" (148) and submits to being caught by God.[9]

Ferlinghetti's *Her* provides an exploration of life and letters on several different levels. His novel becomes his own alembic, a vehicle for refining. The "underivative creation" is achieved through the illusionary narrative of the novel. The "her" being sought is the book being written—*Her*. The relationship between the author, frustrated in his attempt at autobiography, and his created character, prevented from asserting a measure of autonomous independence, symbolizes a view of the human predicament. Ferlinghetti shows man as the inadvertent operator of the machinery of associations, frustrated in his attempts at "underivative creation." As victim of the illusions generated by those associations, man becomes a helpless puppet, energized by clichés and uncontrollable, repetitious behavior. Finally, the latter circumstance is used to portray man's helplessness in the hands of his Creator, with questionable free will and limited spontaneity, destined to re-enact perpetually the eternal movie of man in this world.

Notes

[1]The "it all" of this quote is a film of a "museum of objects depicting the history of my race," a passage which Ferlinghetti reads on the album *Tentative Description* and which appeared in the *San Francisco Review*.

[2]Ferlinghetti has noted that *Her* "fits into the French tradition of the novel. Like you can fit it in the Robbe-Grillet and Breton's *Nadja*" (Meltzer 157).

[3]Among other cinematic allusions, Ferlinghetti refers to the early surrealist film by Luis Buñuel and Salvador Dali, *Un Chien Andalou*; Ferlinghetti uses the phrase "chien d'Andalou" (31, 37). He also includes an anecdote (36-37) apparently based on Roman Polanski's short film *Two Men and a Wardrobe*, an allegory whose theme of frustration is reiterated by Raffine.

[4]*Palimpsest* was originally published in 1926. Ferlinghetti alludes to the work even before Raffine cites his encounter with it in the second section of *Her*. In the first section, Lubin asks Raffine, "Who fished you up, anyway, who fished the murex up?" (66). The latter clause serves as the epigraph to the second story in *Palimpsest*.

[5]Ferlinghetti has generally denied that *Her* is a novel. In the notes on the back cover of the volume, he says that it is a "surreal semi-autobiographical blackbook record." He described it to Judith Serebnick as an "autobiographical romance" (636). He stated in an interview, "It wasn't a novel, it wasn't supposed to be a novel. It was a surrealist notebook that I kept, a Black Book. It is a book which New Directions calls a novel" (Meltzer 157). However, in other interviews he refers to "my novel 'Her'" (*Idiot* 19) and states, "I wrote a novel called *Her*—my Paris novel—" (Selerie 7). His reluctance to classify *Her* as a novel reinforces the conflict between fiction and autobiography.

[6]Robbe-Grillet is discussing his movie *L'Immortelle*.

[7]Stimpson's article examines Ginsberg, Kerouac, and Burroughs, but not Ferlinghetti.

[8]For a discussion of the varied functions of the string in *Her*, see Smith 189.

[9]The clothbound edition of *Her* concludes with the phrase "O god," ambiguously expressing both celebration and exasperation. The phrase was omitted in the paperbound edition. A carbon copy of Ferlinghetti's original 1959 manuscript located in the Bancroft Library, University of California at Berkeley, concludes with the word "god" printed 155 times.

The Poet as Poem

> Such reflections lead me to the conclu-
> sion that criticism, abjuring, it is true,
> its dearest prerogatives but aiming, on
> the whole, at a goal less futile than
> the automatic adjustment of ideas
> should confine itself to scholarly incur-
> sions upon the very realm supposedly
> barred to it, and which, separate from
> the work, is a realm where the author's
> personality, victimized by the petty
> events of daily life, expresses itself
> quite freely and often in so distinctive a
> manner.   (Breton 13)

Among the radical changes of technique and perspective
in the art of the twentieth century, one that is frequently over-
looked is the sociological fact that the situation of the artist has
been altered by the proliferation of the mass media. Artists have
become public to such an extent that their roles and reputations
may easily become their major concerns—and their primary
themes. The use of the first person in poetry traditionally becomes a device for universalization: an experience or sensation
is employed to speak to or reveal a generalized point, embodying
Lautréamont's tenet that "Whoever considers the life of a man
finds therein the history of the species" (340). However, in
much of the poetry of the Beat Generation writers, the personal
and subjective elements become distressingly autistic: everyday
trivia and personal experiences are described, as is frequently the
case in Lawrence Ferlinghetti's poems, to portray and congratu-
late the writer himself. A chief subject of Ferlinghetti's poetry is
often Ferlinghetti himself. The subjective element in the poems
seems calculated to reveal the poet to the reader rather than to
illuminate the reader. The success of his subjective poems is
compromised when Ferlinghetti focuses self-consciously on his
role as poet or on nugatory occasions and indulges in mock self-

deprecation, but more frequently the genuine wit and comfortable presence of his speakers transform personal observations into significant images of the human condition.

Since World War II, the artist has become as important as—if not at times more important than—the work of art. The artist's personality and image are the most important creations. Thus, as A. Alvarez has charged, Dylan Thomas "was under constant pressure from the literary Public Relations Officers to continue at all costs less with his poetry than with his act as the blindly inspired poet" (23). In addition, Salvador Dali promoted his reputation for bizarre behavior and outrageousness, as when he appeared on late night television talk shows or modeled capes in *Esquire* ("Swashbuckling" 106-09). His face, with an exquisitely sculptured moustache, is probably more readily recognizable than all but one or two of his paintings. He has created a commercially successful persona, characterized by eccentricity. Andy Warhol exploited the same propensity—and also satirized it: "'Why is *The Chelsea Girls* art?' [Warhol] inquired, referring to one of his movies. 'Well, first of all, it was made by an artist, and, second, that would come out as art'" (qtd. in Rosenberg 98), unconsciously echoing Robert Frost's "Poetry is the kind of thing poets write." In addition, in 1966 Warhol advertised in a newspaper that he would sign his name to anything brought to him including dollar bills, thus converting these mundane objects into "Art" (Rosenberg 105). Likewise, he has loaned his name, as producer, to movies (*Trash*, among others) and to rock music groups (The Velvet Underground). Warhol's use of a look-alike for personal appearances parodied this personality cult ingeniously. The more unconventional his behavior, the more public attention he would receive. After initial success the artist no longer need produce quality work (or even any work at all), so long as he remains in full view of the public eye.

This situation arises partially because the arts themselves have begun to closely approach the popular media. As the "popular" arts and the "serious" arts become virtually indistinguishable and interchangeable, the serious artists find themselves in the eminently seduceable roles of popular artists and become common property. As a result, their subsequent work, whether in the verbal, plastic, or performing arts, threatens to conform to the role in which they have been cast. The seemingly inevitable result is a diminution or sullying of the quality of their output through repetition and replication, if only to satisfy their constituency—or, at any rate, to avoid the alienation of that constituency. A viable and frequently occurring alternative is for the artists to offer themselves as substitutes for their works of art. Sometimes they, complicitly or inadvertently, find themselves performers within the world of popular art: Truman Capote, Norman Mailer, Jerzy Kosinski, and John Irving have all had bit acting parts in major films; Ferlinghetti appeared reading a poem in the film *The Last Waltz*; Allen Ginsberg toured with Bob Dylan's Rolling Thunder Review, and he has performed onstage with and recorded (on their *Combat Rock* album) with the rock group The Clash; Jack Kerouac is featured as a character in Tom Robbins's novel *Even Cowgirls Get the Blues*, and Ferlinghetti is a character in Richard Brautigan's novel *The Tokyo-Montana Express*. Popularity and public atttention pose severe threats to artists. The quality of their production and the response of established critics to this work become inconsequential—as long as the response is extreme. Thus, a UPI release about the Surrounded Islands project of the artist Christo reveals that "project spokesmen say that reaction—any kind of reaction—is part of the point of the art work" (8 May 1983). In such a case, the very arbiters of artistic taste may await or attempt to anticipate the public verdict. Values grow eclectic until it is not rare to hear someone express enthusiasm for Beethoven *and* the Beatles, Goya *and* Christo, Shakespeare *and* Shepard. The critic finds himself forced either to capitulate or to despair.

The Beat Generation writers have certainly perpetuated this problem, with their primarily subjective criteria. Their supporters have been bulwarks and proselytizers of the "I don't know what's good, but I know what I like" approach to the arts. This attitude, though thoroughly democratic, minimizes the validity of the trained eye of critical evaluation. It preaches that art is not to be understood but to be appreciated as experience. The ultimate criterion is intensity of vision; the truth or falseness of that vision matters less. To a limited degree, this intuitive approach has provided a valuable re-invigoration of the arts, but it has also left them terribly vulnerable to abuse.

Ferlinghetti is one of the most conspicuous practitioners of a new type of poetry designed as an intentional rebuke to what the Beats considered the sterility of academic poetry, what Ferlinghetti has characterized as

> the barren, polished poetry and well-mannered verse which had dominated many of the major poetry publications during the past decade or so, not to mention some of the "fashionable incoherence" which has passed for poetry in many of the smaller, *avant-garde* magazines and little presses. ("Horn on *Howl*" 134)

The new poetry demands that the reader engage it, interact with it, rather than study it (similarly, Bob Dylan once refused to allow his song lyrics to be anthologized in their entirety as poems because he did not want to be studied in the universities). Together with the development of a fresh poetics, a new type of subject matter arrives which is intensely personal and which often focuses sharply and clearly on the poet's sensibilities, what Leslie Fiedler calls "the re-emergence of the 'I' at the center of the poem" (233). However, this poetry is not confessional in the conventional sense. The poet details his everyday actions and reactions so that the poems become a record of his existence.

Ferlinghetti's range here is worth detailing: his subjective poems might well be seen as occasional, but the occasions inspiring them are often nugatory, as though the poet were attempting to illustrate another of Lautréamont's suggestions, that the unusual is to be found in the banal, as he tries "to write out the true poem of my life" ("Genesis" 445). His poem "Truth is not the secret of a few" seems to have resulted from a minor confrontation with either a librarian or an attendant at a museum. The trivial nature of the complaint is reinforced by the conclusion of the poem, where the poet resorts to off-color humor:

> walking around in museums always makes me
>   want to
>   'sit down'
>   I always feel so
>   constipated
>   in those
>   high altitudes. (*Pictures* #9)

Similarly, in "Bickford's Buddha" (*Secret* 11-19), he recounts being evicted from Harvard Library by guards because he has no student identification card. He takes this eviction personally rather than considering its obviously general application. In a puerile and devastating diatribe, *The Illustrated Wilfred Funk*, Ferlinghetti employs a barrage of adolescent and scatalogical bile to condemn the character Funk, presumably redeeming such juvenilia by sudden self-condemnations of identification with Funk. This form of self-castigation also occurs in other poems as the poet mockingly and self-consciously deprecates himself and his artistic creations. Thus, he recalls a night during which a group of writers

> read their worst verse
> (somewhat resembling this).
>> ("Overheard Conversations," *Who* 30)

In his "Populist Manifesto," he provides an indictment of the directions of contemporary poetry and charges himself also: "All you "Poets of the Cities" / hung in museums, including myself" (*Who* 62).[1] In "The Third World," Ferlinghetti calls attention to

> old funnyface
> myself
>> the bargain tragedian. (*Open* 81-82)

Such self-criticism might at first glance seem to suggest that the poet's self-pitying disappointment at his supposed lack of physical beauty manifested itself in an outlook of cheap cynicism— until one recognizes how cleverly the poet has managed to link images of the conventional masks of comedy and tragedy.

Artistically damaging, however, are instances when the persona feels his poetic stature threatened. Ferlinghetti, who has described himself as "a poet against my will" ("Genesis" 445), incorporates his consciousness of and concern with his poetic role and reputation into the poems themselves. In "Bickford's Buddha" the poet visits the Harvard Co-op and hears a girl ask for "books by Ferlinghetti"; with the rather forced humor of colloquial spelling and grammar, he adds parenthetically, "They dint have none" (*Secret* 11). Later, he passes the Grolier Bookshop, where photographs hang of the poets who have passed there. Because his own picture is not among them, he whines,

> Where am I
> walking by
> not announcing meself
> Phooey I'm a poet too. (*Secret* 13)

Here again non-standard grammar attempts to mask the wounded pride of the speaker.   In "Mock Confessional" he self-
consciously says, "Anyway I hear people are wondering about
me / and I've written this to clear the air" (*Open* 6).   In *Back
Roads to Far Places*, he imagines himself aging:

> I'll be a strange wild
> wandering old man
> thought by some
> to be a sage.

On such occasions, self-aggrandizement can result in the embar-
rassment of poetic posturing.   In "Autobiography" he gushes in
celebration of his own creativity:

> I am a hill
> where poets run.
> ....
> I am a hill of poetry.
> ....
> For I am a still
> of poetry.
> I am a bank of song. (*Coney* 65; ellipses supplied)

Sometimes a single evaluative adjective accounts for the
disconcerting impression of the poet's self-applause. In "Holiday
Inn Blues," the narrator sits in a bar "Making up fantastic
fictional histories" (*Landscapes* 18) of two of the customers.
After a series of sexual-religious puns in "Mock Confessional,"
the speaker describes his jokes as "bright cocktail chatter" (*Open*
7).   "The Love Nut" (*Landscapes* 16-17) depends entirely upon
inverted self-congratulation: the narrator examines himself in a
mirror and in mock castigation derides himself for his healthy,
humane values.   "Director of Alienation" (*Who* 6-9), also opening with the speaker's sight of himself in a mirror, employs the
very same tactic.
     Closely connected with this self-concern are examples of
the poet bewailing the demands made of him precisely because
he is an artist.   The result, of course, is obliquely self-
congratulatory: the poet compliments himself by regretting the
implications of his talent.[2] Thus, when Ferlinghetti states,

> Some days I'm afflicted
> with Observation Fever

> omnivorous perception of phenomena
> not just visual, ("Bickford's Buddha," *Secret* 11)

the pose is that of the artist saying, "Look at me, a poet, looking at things," and the poetic middleman is not easily dismissed, for he becomes the essence of the poem. Ferlinghetti returns to the observer role often, feeling he is

> really afflicted
> with this observation biz
> It never stops
> on & on & on. ("Bickford's Buddha," *Secret* 12)

In a perceptive essay, Sally M. Gall examines a related tendency in contemporary poetry, "which frequently reduces to 'me talking to you about me—my thoughts, my feelings, my experiences,'" and in which she discovers a "preoccupation with the trivialities of day-to-day existence" and a "Stevensian 'Watch Me Thinking' air" (491). The stance is one which Ferlinghetti repeatedly adopts. As Wordsworth does in this preface to *Lyrical Ballads*, Ferlinghetti emphasizes the poet's ability to see more clearly than the ordinary man, and, to be sure, observation of the details of the world is artistically crucial. However, the difference between the description of this quality and the self-pluming of a man who claims to possess it is disturbing. Arrogance and effrontery do not contribute to the creation of a persona with whom the reader can feel comfortable. Camping out in the wilderness in "Reading Apollinaire by the Rogue River," Ferlinghetti's narrative voice exclaims, "And I see the Rogue for real / as the Indians saw him" (*Landscapes* 52). One is reminded of D. H. Lawrence's *Studies in Classic American Literature* with its criticism of Whitman for this type of encompassing presumption (166 ff.). A comparison of sections from two poems can illuminate the problem: in the second of Ferlinghetti's "Canti Romani," the narrator claims,

> I could still hear the gladiators
> yelling at their horses
> and the cries of the warriors and martyrs
> being run through
> with spears and long swords
> mixed with the cries of taxi drivers
>   and tour guides (*Over All* 67);

in "History of the World: A TV Docu-Drama," he makes a similar trans-historical assertion: near Santa Fe

> you can almost hear
> the cracks of whips over horses
> the cries of the drivers in the rising dust. (*Over All* 115)

In the latter case, the use of the second person pronoun generalizes the observation and reduces the possible impression of the poet applauding himself for special powers of perception.

Ferlinghetti celebrates his own perception as the mystical third eye vision, his "blue blue eyes / which see as one eye / in the middle of the head" ("True Confessional," *Open* 5). He smugly disparages a fellow passenger on a boattrain for what he assumes must be insensitivity:

> That fellow on the boattrain who insisted
> on playing blackjack
> had teeth that stuck out
> like lighthouses on a rocky coast
>
> but
> he had no eyes to see
> the dusk flash past
> horses in orchards
> noiselessly running
> bunches of birds
> thrown up
> and the butterflies of yesterday
> that flittered on
> my mind. (*Pictures* #20)

The effect is one of aesthetic superiority, and the preening self-inflation is grating. Similarly, in "The Living Theatre," the poet's objectivity approaches insensitivity, a tendency reinforced by the adjective used to describe the lives of those he observes:

> I do not laugh and cry with them
> I am just their dramaturge
> or some foreign theatre critic
> come to see the spectacle
> of their little lives played out. (*Over All* 98)

The impression conveyed is not one of artistic observation but of arrogant snobbery.

In several poems Ferlinghetti clearly adopts a voice intended to express a point of view antithetical to his own. In "One Thousand Fearful Words for Fidel Castro," he employs what Samuel Charters calls the "rhetorical technique . . . of the pretended fool" (78) in order to reveal the shallowness and hypocrisy of an ultra-nationalistic American unsympathetic to Castro. The criticisms are hyperbolic and parodistic, until the conclusion, where the poet finally offers an endorsement of Castro's overthrow of Cuban oppression: "I give you my sprig of laurel" (*Starting* 52).[3] The complexity of the problem of voice increases when one recognizes the allusions in the last stanza of the poem to Whitman's celebrations of Lincoln and the concluding line as a variant of "I give you my sprig of lilac," from "When Lilacs Last in the Dooryard Bloom'd" (234). Similarly, "Highway Patrol" becomes an exercise in impersonation, speaking through the persona of a bigoted, vulgar, and violent "redneck" California patrolman; the poem concludes with a phrase identifying both the source of the personna's values and the source of Ferlinghetti's stereotyped portrait: "Just like in the movies" (*Who* 38). In "The Pied Piper of Iron Mountain," the speaker is a businessman from "the suburbs of Pittsburgh," with "steely" eyes and "iron progeny," who leads the children of the future into "the black mouth of Iron Mountain," away from what "once was a garden called Earth" (*Landscapes* 11).

Many of Ferlinghetti's poems are verbal photographs, and the presence of a subjective quality, even if it serves only in the capacity of a commenting observer, prevents these poems from becoming flat still lifes and injects an experiential dimension. Often this dimension is necessary to maintain a realistic referent in the midst of surreal poetic fantasy. Thus, "Overpopulation" projects a futuristic society which is tempered by the narrator's hesitation, aroused by the hole in the newspaper he is reading: "I must have misunderstood something / in this story" (*Starting* 28), he suggests, anticipating and disarming the reader's own skepticism. Many of Ferlinghetti's poems, including "Yes" (*Pictures* #7), "The pennycandystore beyond the El" (*Coney* 35), "Starting from San Francisco" (*Starting* 5-8), and "Overpopulation" (*Starting* 28-32), face the reader with impressionistic and/or surrealistic materials, and the first-person presence provides a solidity and integrity which allow the poems to partake of natural human fantasy rather than to remain formal poetic constructs.

Ferlinghetti's subjective poems are most successful when
the speaker is employed as a self-effacing, comfortable presence
generating wit and warmth. The poet's preoccupation with his
creative role can even be presented capably in these circumstances:

>   Yet I have slept with beauty
>   in my own weird way
>   and I have made a hungry scene or two
>   with beauty in my bed
>   and so spilled out another poem or two
>   and so spilled out another poem or two
>   upon the Bosch-like world.
>   ("I have not lain with beauty all my life," *Coney* 24)

Here the modest choice of the word "spilled" lends the assertion
the grace of humility and affords an escape from the charge of
artistic egotism. "Autobiography" offers a generalized portrait
tempered with ironic humor, beginning with a sad and disap-
pointed American childhood:

>   I looked homeward
>   and saw no angel.
>   I got caught stealing pencils
>   from the Five and Ten Cent Store
>   the same month I made Eagle Scout. (*Coney* 60)

The narrator goes on to describe the unfair and debilitating social
conditions of modern America, which he assures the reader that
he has witnessed, in an echo of Whitman's passage from "Song
of Myself," "I am the man, I suffer'd, I was there" (51):

>   I have seen them.
>   I am the man.
>   I was there.
>   I suffered
>   somewhat. (*Coney* 64)

The effect of the word "somewhat," its surprise heightened by
the line break, provides a wry deflation of what could have been
pomposity or sentimentality. An entry in *Northwest Ecolog* (14)
employs a similar technique:

>   A fifteen year old boy drowned here yesterday / swept away by the
>   undercurrent / his boots on / sucked into a deep hole / We found a

> striped T-shirt and a pair of canvas shoes upon a beach downriver /
> Looked more like girls' shoes but might have been boys' if he were
> slightly androgynous / We turned them over to the county sheriff /
> who came zooming downriver / in a tin boat / with his emblem
> emblazoned on the bow / We didn't mention androgyny.

The control here is so tight and tough-minded that it threatens to err on the side of callousness.

Subjective poems set in specific dramatic situations require a focus on details which enables them to avoid the weaknesses of posturing and self-indulgence. Ferlinghetti's "Great American Waterfront Poem" (*Who* 34-36) and "In a Time of Revolution For Instance" (*Open* 10-12) are particularly effective examples. In the former poem, the narrator finds himself in a situation increasingly familiar in America in the last half of the twentieth century: he is awaiting a phone call about his divorce decree. He finds himself on the "waterfront of existence," on the edge of land's stability, facing the treacherous freedom of the ocean. Furthermore, the narrator's personal feelings are mixed: he sees himself in a "divorce from civilization," in a classic struggle of Eros and Civilization, echoing the forces drawn by Marcuse, but he also fears that his gesture is futile, that "there isn't any longer any Away."[4] The poem is filled with personal tension, apprehension, and anxiety; it concludes realistically with a refusal to supply a facile resolution: "The tide is at the ebb The phone rings." The poem's success stems largely from its sympathetic portrait of an idealistic, vulnerable narrator, a man with more questions than answers, who sees, in convincing fashion, the helplessness of his own situation as applicable to the general human condition in an age when one cannot even expect Matthew Arnold's romantic fidelity after the Sea of Faith has begun to ebb. "In a Time of Revolution, For Instance" paints with telling perception the ambivalent response of a "have-not" confronted with representatives of the world of upper-class style. The mixed feelings of attraction and repulsion assert themselves immediately:

> I don't know how or why I
> thought they must be
> fucked-up except
> they were very beautiful. (*Open* 10)

The detailed attention of the narrator to the appearance, man-
ners, and behavior of the three "beautiful" people reveals the
narrator's begrudging fascination. He recognizes the vast social
and economic chasm that separates them from himself, and the
epiphanic moment discloses his dissatisfaction with his own
status, symbolized by his fishplate lunch:

> my fish finally arrived looking
> not quite unfrozen and
> quite plastic. (12)

Nevertheless, he admits, "I decided to eat it anyway," as he
realizes that the good life, as attractive and elegant as it appears,
is regrettably beyond his grasp. He resigns himself to the bleakness of his own world but allows himself the luxury of pipe
dreams.

The success of these poems resides in the naturalness of
the first-person voice, articulate in its depiction and development of specific situations, registering a middle range of life's
common disappointments. The poems point no finger at specific villains: all are victims or potential victims. More importantly, the best of the subjective poems owe their mastery to the
particular focus of perception, concentrating on the objects of
observation rather than on the speaker's act of observation, thus
revealing the narrator's character indirectly. In the introduction
to his translation of Jacques Prévert's poems, Ferlinghetti
applauds the French poet:

> Still there are many so-called poets around these days who have
> need of such a seeing-eye dog in the street. Prévert remains a great
> 'see-er' if not a great seer. He writes as one talks while walking,
> and 'la poésie est dans la démarche.' His ubiquitous eye enumerates
> the ordinary world with a 'movement transfigurateur.' (5)

The same praise can be offered to Ferlinghetti in his subjective
poems—as long as that ubiquitous eye is not turned in upon
itself. The "I" of the best of these poems provides a comfortable
companion on those walks, a Virgil-like guide pointing to the
familiar and the unfamiliar and discovering something to be
marvelled at in everything perceived.

Notes

[1]The allusion apparently involves Ferlinghetti's inclusion in a Dallas-organized 1974-75 exhibition entitled "Poets of the Cities New York and San Francisco 1950-1965."

[2]Jack Kerouac indulges in similar affectation: in *On the Road*, Dean presses Sal about his writing, and Sal replies,

> Hell, man, I know very well you didn't come to me only to want to become a writer, and after all what do I really know about it except that you've got to stick to it with the energy of a benny addict. (7)

[3]Ferlinghetti eventually rejected Castro's increasingly dictatorial control:

> In the history of revolutions, the issue of individual civil rights and especially freedom of speech and press has been the pivot upon which all in the end has stood or fallen. So it was in Cuba—to the dismay of many early supporters; so it will be in Nicaragua—whose leaders are trying valiantly, it would seem, to avoid the mistakes Cuba made.
> . . . .
> The Revolution is being directed by a group—there is no single dictator, no dictatorship except of "the people." (I'd heard that before—in Havana in 1960-61—in the early euphoric stages of the Cuban Revolution, before their revolution became institutionalized—or sovietized. (*Seven Days*)

[4]Ferlinghetti's assertion appears to echo Rupert Birkin's pronouncement that "There *is* no away" in D. H. Lawrence's *Women in Love* (238). Many of Ferlinghetti's poems reflect his interest in the themes and symbols of Lawrence, most obviously, of course, in "The Man Who Rode Away" (*Open* 34-36), which is specifically dedicated to Lawrence.

"Constantly Risking Absurdity"

In 1957, Lawrence Ferlinghetti and Kenneth Rexroth participated in a series of experiments in a San Francisco night club, The Cellar, where the two writers read their poetry to live jazz accompaniment. These experiments were not entirely successful: Ferlinghetti comments, "Nothing was worse than most of the poetry and jazz in the fifties. Most of it was awful. The poet ended up sounding like he was hawking fish from a street corner. All the musicians wanted to do was blow. Like, 'Man, go ahead and read your poems but we gotta blow'" (Meltzer 169). However, the importance of these jazz-poetry experiments cannot be ignored: the poets—and the audiences of these readings— were straining against the restrictions of the printed page. At that time, the Beats were condemning conventional poetry as "square," academic in the worst sense of the word. Jazz suggested a new direction, with one of its most attractive features being its improvisatory quality.

The sources of the poetry-music tradition spring from primitive word-chants and continue through the wandering minstrels and troubadours. The *café chantant* offered another model, as did the Italian *commedia dell'arte improviso*, which provided many of the same attractions as jazz. In addition, the spontaneous quality of the American talking-blues was undoubtedly also influential. Ferlinghetti acknowledges Vachel Lindsay and Carl Sandburg as forerunners of this mode of expression:

> And the poets don't write their poem with the idea of its being read aloud in mind when they write it. Poetry used to have an audience. Lindsay went around the country reciting poems for bread —that was his phrase. And Sandburg, when he was younger, went around with a guitar and had an audience. (quoted in Gleason)

Thus, the Beat coupling of poetry with contemporary music was a timely rebirth of a popular tradition.

The most important aspect to emerge from these experiments was the attention which centered on the sound of literature. As Lawrence Lipton points out, "Many poets had forgotten that poetry *has* a sound" (221). In addition, modern technology influenced this focus: "When the Library of Congress began its recorded poetry series, many poets, confronted suddenly with the request that they read their work aloud, found themselves tongue-tied and self-conscious to the point of physical distress" (221). The very availability and accessibility of sound recording equipment was a major spur toward reconsideration of poetry's sound. This oral emphasis has, in many ways, been beneficial to the art of poetry. However, its drawbacks are also of considerable significance, especially because of the temptation for the poet to depend upon delivery in the same way a comedian does. As a result, "one-liners," puns, and other forms of humor may replace the meat of the poem as the distinction between the poet and the popular entertainer begins to diminish. Newer but cheaper poetic standards and values may become entrenched as the poet assigns increasing importance to the immediate response of the audience. This is not, of course, the inevitable and universal response, but the temptations of the footlights can never be easily ignored.

For many of the Beat writers, the sound patterns of literature are central concerns. In 1958, Ferlinghetti commented on the importance of sound in communicating poetry to an audience: "The big thing is the oral message. My whole kick has been oral poetry. The poets today are talking to themselves, they have no other audience" (quoted in Gleason). Since early in his career, Ferlinghetti has written poetry which was intentionally designed to be accompanied by music: his note accompanying the "Oral Messages" section of *A Coney Island of the Mind* explains, "These seven poems were conceived specifically for jazz accompaniment and as such should be considered as spontaneously spoken 'oral messages' rather than as poems written for the printed page" (48). Therefore, in these poems (with the exception of the conclusion of "Dog"), he abandons his idiosyncratic line graphics. In addition, the very title of one of the seven, "Junkman's Obbligato," serves notice of the importance of musical accompaniment. However, Ferlinghetti wavers in his allegiance to the musical impulse: "Let the poet carry it, if he can. He shouldn't have to join the American Federation of

Musicians to make it. Even though a natural affinity does exist between the 'protest poet' and the jazz musician who blows 'dissent on the horn'" (Jacket notes). Nevertheless, he repeatedly returns to musical forms: "Assassination Raga" (*Secret* 3-10) was first read to the accompaniment of a loud raga, and the poem's incrementally repeated phrases provide a verbal parallel to the improvised variations and progressions and the melodic formulas and patterns of the traditional Hindu musical form; *Open Eye, Open Heart* includes a dozen works in a section entitled "American Mantra & Songs"; and the first two sections of *A Trip to Italy & France* are titled respectively "Canti Romani" and "Canti Toscani." Ferlinghetti admits to being of two minds about musical adjunction and notes that for outdoor readings

> the single unaccompanied voice can't make it in that kind of setting. Unless you have an instrument to back up your voice, like Allen Ginsberg uses a harmonium. As soon as you have an instrument, a guitar or autoharp, or harmonium, you can make it outdoors. But a discursive poem that requires concentration is practically always lost outdoors. People are wandering around and talking, it's the open air. There's a contradiction in saying that poetry should be in the street because in the street the poetry is murdered.
>
> (Codrescu Interview 35)

Nevertheless, whether his poems are designed as songs or not, the emphasis on oral quality is maintained, with musical structure continuing as an informing principle, for, as he asserts, in "Modern Poetry Is Prose (But It Is Saying Plenty)," "It is the bird singing that makes us happy" (*Endless* 209).

Frequently Ferlinghetti's typographical delineation manages to convey musical structure, as the patterns the lines take on the printed page reflect the swing of the rhythm, rebelling against the arbitrary rule of justifying each line at the left hand margin. Instead, Ferlinghetti freely utilizes the space of the page to graph the measure. He is particularly adept at employing simple devices to control and manipulate the pace of his poems. In "Not too long," the lines stumble along lazily and sporadically until, in a sudden frantic passage designed to show the self-indulgence of a populace which ignores its artists, the poem provides an accumulative and hastened speed:

> and about
> one hundredandsixtythree people all talking and waving and

> laughing and eating and drinking and smiling and frowning and
> shaking heads and opening mouths and putting forks and spoons in
> them and chewing and swallowing all kinds of produce and sitting
> back and relaxing maybe and drinking coffee and lighting ciga-
> rettes and getting up and so on. (*Pictures* #5)

The very next poem in that first collection changes speed in the
opposite direction. The poem opens in a run-on flurry:

> And the Arabs asked terrible questions
> and the Pope didn't know what to say and the people ran around in
> wooden shoes asking which way was the head of Midas facing and
> everyone said....

Gradually the action and images decelerate until coming to a
virtual halt:

> and then the pool was very
>   still. (*Pictures* #6)

The word "still" stands virtually isolated on the page, as form
effectively reflects content. Ferlinghetti sometimes also employs
heightened forms of typography to supply his emphases: words
and even whole lines may be capitalized or italicized, as though
the poet were uncertain of his ability to supply the requisite force
and impact through verbal structure and syntax. The emphasized words thus become the print equivalent of increased vocal
volume, a form of artificial emphasis rather like that of a person
shouting to make a point. On occasion, the print emphasis can
provide unusual effects. In "Fortune" (*Pictures* #11), the capitalized "FIREMEN" effectively captures the dramatized excite-
ment of the child's perception as the firemen spray their hoses
into the hot air of a summer day. In "London," capitalization
highlights verbal tensions:

> and I must say she did look
>   a bit
>   ASTOUNDED. (*Pictures* #18)

The description "a bit" is inappropriate for the intensity of the
word "astounded": the use of upper-case letters serves to exag-
gerate that unsuitability. Ferlinghetti also uses typography to provide emblematic form in shaping several of his poems. "Dove
sta amore" (*Coney* 43) and "Come Lie with Me and Be My Love"

(*Starting* 36) each assume the shape of gravestone epitaphs, the form providing a grimly ironic commentary on the poems. His very first poem, "Away above a harborful" (*Pictures* #1), with its staggered lines, roughly mimics the shape of the clothes hanging on washlines, which constitute the central image. Ferlinghetti has also dabbled in concrete poetry in "Concrete Politics" (*Open* 73) and uses poetic form to mimic action in "*Johnny Nolan has a patch on his ass*":

                like

                a
             ball
                bounced
                    down steps. (*Coney* 37)

Several of Ferlinghetti's books express a further concern with typographic power: *Tyrannus Nix?*, *Back Roads to Far Places*, *Love Is No Stone on the Moon*, and *The Illustrated Wilfred Funk* abandon conventional type in favor of the poet's own calligraphic script, designed to offer a more personalized format, and the middle two of these volumes also incorporate artwork by the poet himself.

    The Beats saw jazz as a predominantly colloquial medium, its spontaneity and improvisation suggesting personal freedom rather than formal confinement, and their poetry modeled on jazz attempts to project the same qualities. Vocabulary and grammatical structure in Ferlinghetti's poems are popular rather than formal, vernacular rather than academic, as the poet attempts to create a form of oral expression which accurately reflects contemporary spoken American English. As Larry Smith points out, "American culture as it is reflected in common speech is both a subject and a method in his oral messages" (80). Slang, vulgarities, and idiomatic expressions all season the themes of the poems. Colloquialisms, by definition, contribute to the oral quality of the poems because they are essentially spoken constructs. On occasion, Ferlinghetti's usage of informal language and non-standard grammar is forced and self-conscious, but generally it effectively embodies his material. His orthographic variations attempt to phonetically capture casual American pronunciation by means of eye dialect:

> Get a loada this junk
> You wanna belong
> You gotta have it. ("Director of Alienation," *Who* 8-9)

In his notes to "Las Vegas Tilt," he explains his use of the word "'Southren'—dialect spelling, as pronounced, southeastern United States."[1]   Nonstandard grammatical syntax is frequently utilized to reflect unrefined, spontaneous, colloquial usage, particularly in the lack of formal subject-verb agreement and the double negatives: "He don't wanna be alone" ("The Love Nut," *Landscapes* 16); "There won't be no real revolution" ("Underwear," *Starting* 35).   Conversational patterns of language usage also contribute to the oral quality of the poems: in "Not too long" (*Pictures* #5), the colloquial transitional marker "but anyway" appears three times.   Familiar conversational tail-offs are also in evidence:

> and not barking
>   or waving its funny tail or
>   anything
>   ("And the Arabs asked terrible questions," *Pictures* #6);

> took up television and crosswords
>   even crocheting
>   and things like that.
>   ("And she 'like a young year," *Pictures* #12)

The final filler phrases in these passages are non-functional in written language, but common in oral usage.   Most impressive, however, is Ferlinghetti's use of the vocabulary of popular culture, particularly the jazz-Beat-hip patois.   In a remarkable tour de force, "Sometime during eternity" (*Coney* 15-16), he retells the life of Christ in "hip" idiom, similar to Lord Buckley's version, "The Naz."[2]   The poem works in two directions, celebrating two distinctly creative languages which communicate a fundamental theme and revealing the persistence of this theme, gem-precious to every artist, of the messenger of light and love in a world of Philistines.   Similarly, the shared humanity of common language is demonstrated in the poem "funny fantasies are never so real as oldstyle romances," where Ferlinghetti limns a portrait of a sophisticated woman whose pose is convincingly destroyed as she speaks the last two lines of the poem to her equally dignified romancer:

                    Let's lie down somewheres
                              baby. (*Pictures* #15)

The colloquial forms provide the verisimilitude of conversational language and give the themes the flavor of generalized
truth.

    With Ferlinghetti's emphasis on sound, auditory figures
of speech, especially alliteration, assonance, and consonance
(often in combinations), are carefully developed. The opening
and conclusion of "Moscow in the Wilderness, Segovia in the
Snow" demonstrate his skill in interweaving consonant and
vowel sounds in recurrent patterns:

          Midnight Moscow Airport
                  sucks me in from Siberia
          And blows me out alone
                          in a black bus
                  down dark straight night roads
                  stark snow plains
                          eternal taiga
                              into monster Moscow
              stands of white birches
                  ghosted in the gloaming
          ....
          unglues its great gut mouth
                  and utters
                          ecstatic static. (*Secret* 40, 48)

At times the control of sound patterns is so refined that words
and phrases seem to interlock with each other, as in the poem
"Away above a harborful":

              while in the reachless seascape spaces
                      between the blown white shrouds
                  stand out the bright steamers
                          to kingdom come. (*Pictures* #1)

However, Ferlinghetti sometimes seems seduced by the siren
song of sound patterns into allowing those patterns to control
the movement or direction of his poems: "And hung up His
holy hair" ("Hairy Man" 133); "While I always dreamed of
Afghanistan banana stands" ("Overheard Conversations," *Who*
26); "Toulouse-Lautrec of Lucca" ("Canti Toscani III," *Over All*
83). In each case here, the poet seems more interested in the
shell than in the kernel of meaning. Such instances leave Fer-

linghetti vulnerable to the charge D. H. Lawrence brought against Edgar Allan Poe:

> The absence of real central or impulsive being in himself leaves him inordinately, mechanically sensitive to sounds and effects, associations of sounds, associations of rhyme, for example— mechanical, facile, having no root in any passion. It is all a secondary, meretricious process. (*Studies* 77)

Fortunately, many of Ferlinghetti's effects do not sink to this level; at their best they reinforce meaning and create phrases that are striking and memorable: he describes the Greek sculptor Praxiteles as working "in visible syllables" ("In hintertime Praxiteles," *Pictures* #3); he sees Goya's *Disasters of War* "in an abstract landscape of blasted trees" ("In Goya's greatest scenes we seem to see," *Coney* 9); he imagines Greek refugees "chanting Athenian anthems" ("Sailing thru the straits of Demos," *Coney* 11). A delicate passage in a later poem uses the repetition of vowel and consonant sounds to create an onomatopoeic effect:

> lightly singing
> > a muted melody
> lightly humming
> > to himself
> > > a fretted threnody
> lightly treading
> > the tiled balconies
> the marble terraces
> The swallows
> > swirl about him
> With the dawn they dart away.
> > ("Canti Romani IV," *Over All* 69)

The aural quality of these devices can be deliberately evoked even when they are concealed from the eye: "the wrong rail" ("Just as I used to say," *Pictures* #2); "jungle gym" ("Into Darkness, In Granada," *Open* 43); "jass and gyzm" ("Endless Life," *Endless* 211). Ferlinghetti also delights in the opposite effect: "sweet swaying sword" ("Frightened," *Coney* 33); "nylon nympho" ("Home Home Home," *Landscapes* 33); "leather leashes" ("Canti Romani VIII," *Over All* 77). Here words have the visual appearance of alliteration and/or assonance, but normal pronunciation betrays this expectation.

Ferlinghetti also uses multi-syllabic sound echoes, rhymes, and refrain to reinforce the oral quality of his poems. The sound echoes function by providing similar verbal sequences with only slight variations of pronunciation, either in immediate juxtaposition or in parallel grammatical structure:

> of a cancerous dancer
> "Dada would have liked a day like this," *Pictures* #23);
>
> across the landscape—
>   land escape—
>   ("Through the Looking Glass," *Secret* 28);
>
> Yes yes the world turns and turns on its fascist axis
>   ("A World Awash with Fascism and Fear," *Open* 87);
>
>   pressed an inedible mushroom button
> and an inaudible Sunday bomb
>   fell down
>   ("In a surrealist year," *Coney* 14);
>
> Here now
>   where now
>   is the sea's urge still
> sea's surge and thunder.
> ("The Sea and Ourselves at Cape Ann," *Landscapes* 6)

Ferlinghetti uses these devices for a variety of purposes, ranging from the sharpening of thematic purpose to the injection of humor into a poem. An especially intriguing example of this device appears in "Away above a harborful":

>   she tosses back her head
>   in voiceless laughter
>   and in choiceless gesture then
>   shakes out gold hair
> while in the reachless seascape spaces. (*Pictures* #1)

The words "voiceless," "choiceless," and "reachless" establish a basic melodic pattern, supplanting conventional rhyme, and "seascape spaces" collapses a related substitution into two consecutive words.

Ferlinghetti does on occasion employ rhymes, almost always disastrously: too often they are puerile, manipulated, and facile, creating childishly sing-song effects without offering a childlike grace of innocence and without contributing substance or delight. His rhymes are sporadic (although they appear with much more frequency in *A Trip to Italy & France*), usually occurring at the conclusion of poems. Robert Peters has pointed to Ferlinghetti's "consciously tacky end-rhymes, rendered in a music-hall manner" (26), and they are indeed most successful when serving a comic purpose. Particularly engaging in this vein are the multi-syllabic rhymes:

> Let us arise and go now
> into the interior
> of Foster's Cafeteria
> ("Junkman's Obbligato," *Coney* 58);

> in life's slick chariot
> of the sun
> Judas Iscariot
> on the run. ("Las Vegas Tilt,"*Open* 97)

Such ryhymes provide the element of surprise, often by incorporating foreign words or proper names:

> and I spied her
> through the Italian lattice
> smiling so fatally at him
> and then kissing him
> *gratis*
> ("Snapshot Epiphany," *Who* 23);

> The horses the horses the wild horses at dawn
> as in a watercolor by Ben Shahn
> ("Horses at Dawn," *Endless* 167);

> Sons of Whitman sons of Poe
> sons of Lorca & Rimbaud
> ("Adieu à Charlot (Second Populist Manifesto)," *Landscapes* 41);

> which caused a single bird to fly over
> from the gardens of *Julien-le-pauvre*.
> ("Darkness, Chez George Whitman," *Over All* 26)

Ferlinghetti frequently uses rhymes to underscore (or shape) parallel constructions:

> The blood falls upon those
> from whom it is bled

from whom it is wrung
The blood falls upon those
about whom the song is sung
("A World Awash with Fascism and Fear," *Open* 88-89);

And each insolent gesture
which that body makes
and each arrogant pose
that body takes.
("At the Bodega," *Who* 21)

The latter examples tremble on the edge of lyricism, threatening to topple over into artificiality and manipulation.

Refrains function in Ferlinghetti's poems in several guises, particularly in his longer poems. He employs variations on the classical oratorical device of anaphora, repetition of phrases at the beginning of literary units, in order to impose structure on extended elements. The phrases offer formulaic patterns which gather strength and power through accumulation. After an opening variant line, the next dozen strophes of "Tentative Description of a Dinner To Promote the Impeachment of President Eisenhower" (*Starting* 41-44) begin with the phrase "And after it became obvious," as the poet marshals the evidence to support his argument. "The Old Italians Dying" (*Landscapes* 1-4) and "Rough Song of Animals Dying" (*Landscapes* 54-56) provide this kind of repetition more sporadically, here of the phrases "You have seen them" and "In a dream within a dream I dreamt a dream," to reinforce the elegiac situations of the poems. Especially interesting is the occurrence of a variable anaphora, in which the controlling passages undergo modifications. "Junkman's Obbligato" (*Coney* 54-59) begins with a simple "Let's go" and then introduces each subsequent stanza with variations, even drawing in allusions to the opening lines of familiar modern poems by Yeats and Eliot: "Let us arise and go now" and "Let us go then you and I." Similarly, the central section of "An Elegy on the Death of Kenneth Patchen" (*Open* 37-39) provides a series of quotations from the works of the dead poet, each introduced by a variant of the initial phrase, "And still we hear him say," and the repetitions generate an emotionally charged liturgical quality. More closely approximating the conventional refrain, each stanza of "I Am Waiting" (*Coney* 49-53) concludes with the phrase "rebirth of wonder," until the last, where, surprising the reader's conditioned expectation, the

phrase is exalted into "a renaissance of wonder." More irregularly, "Tentative Description . . ." concludes five of its strophes
with the phrase "from which there was no escape—except
Peace," and "Assassination Raga" (*Secret* 3-10) is punctuated by
the Sufi chant "*La illaha el lill Allah.*" Ferlinghetti frequently
uses a form of repetend, in which variations of a phrase or
phrases recur irregularly within a stanza or poem. In the central
strophe of "Special Clearance Sale of Famous Masterpieces"
(*Starting* 45-47), the phrase "pondering the insoluble problem"
appears eleven times in irregularly spaced and structured forms.
"In the course of human events" appears as the concluding line
of the first three stanzas of "One Thousand Fearful Words for
Fidel Castro" (*Starting* 48-52) before being quoted in its context in
the opening of the American Declaration of Independence, thus
establishing the foundation for its satiric reappearance later in
the poem. In the Kenneth Patchen elegy, the clause "though he
spoke much of love" appears twice before being modified to
"though we speak much of love," then returning to the original.
"They were putting up the statue" (*Coney* 17-18) employs the
repetition of an allusion to Keats's "La Belle Dame sans Merci"
("no bird sang"), which once recognized reveals another level of
irony in the poem. Certainly one of the most adventurous uses
of repetition occurs in "Assassination Raga" in connection with
the "*La illaha el lill Allah*" refrain. The first time this line
appears it is immediately followed by the translation "There is
no god but God"; at its next appearance the verity of the line is
questioned, and the poet alters it: "There is no god but God? /
There is no god but Death." At the next appearance of the Sufi
chant, only the altered statement accompanies it. As though his
cynicism wavers momentarily the poet offers no translation
when the chant appears a fourth time, but, apparently having
resolved the problem by the fifth, he again repeats, "There is no
god but Death." Six more times the chant recurs alone; then
after recognizing the sound of a sitar as the artist's impulse
toward healthy values, the poet varies the translation a final
time: "There is no god but Life." In this poem, the variant forms
provided by the repetend dynamically illustrate the changing
attitudes of the poet as he attempts to cope with the perennial
problem of the apparent triumph of evil over good, of the forces
of darkness over the spirit of light.

Other areas of Ferlinghetti's use of repetition are less salutary. He has a tendency to become enamored of certain images, returning to them on multiple occasions. Thus, "prairie schooners into Pullmans," symbolizing the onward movement of civilization, appears in "Starting from San Francisco" (*Starting* 7), "After the Cries of the Birds" (*Secret* 33), "Heads and Drums" (*Mule* #5), and "History of the World: A TV Docu-Drama" (*Over All* 115); "the cat with future feet" recurs in "What could she say to the fantastic foolybear" (*Coney* 19), "The Great Chinese Dragon" (*Starting* 39), and "The Jack of Hearts (*Who* 1). Such reduplication of imagery becomes sluggishly self-applauding and antithetical to the creative spirit of poetry. A similar problem manifests itself when the poet employs subject-verb or verb-object forms which repeat their root words: "and while the lookers kept looking" ("They were putting up the statue," *Coney* 17), "with its sharp shadows shadowing" ("In woods where many rivers run," *Coney* 34), "painters painting" ("The Billboard Painters," *Landscapes* 29), "White searchlights / search the sky" ("White on White," *Landscapes* 37), "In a dream within a dream I dreamt a dream" ("Rough Song of Animals Dying," *Landscapes* 54), "For there is no end to the hopeful choices / still to be chosen" ("Endless Life," *Endless* 214). Clearly, several of these usages are intended to be humorous, but a dominant effect is one of poverty of vocabulary. Ferlinghetti also uses exact replication of phrases, presumably in order to achieve a lyrical tone. At times the device works effectively for dramatic emphasis, as in the concluding repetition of "Too soon!" in "The pennycandystore beyond the El" (*Coney* 35), and in the final "none returning / none returning" of "Reading Apollinaire by the Rogue River" (*Landscapes* 53). The device is also affecting when applied incrementally as Ferlinghetti uses it in his later works, although overuse diminishes its power. Occasionally the pattern involves the insertion of an adjective in a repeated phrase: "The majesty the sad majesty," "the clouds the furled clouds . . ." ("The Majesty," *Landscapes* 8), "The sea / the lapping sea" ("A Sweet Flying Dream," *Landscapes* 25), "of the sound the hushed sound" ("Canti Romani IV," *Over All* 69). At other times, an adverb may be replaced: "so slightly so lightly" ("Seeing a Woman as in a Painting by Berthe Morisot," *Over All* 209); "looking blindly looking dumbly" ("Scene from a Street Opera," *Over All* 55). Stripped down to mere repetition, the tech-

nique seems reiteratively manipulative: "And the woman the
woman" ("Short Story on a Painting of Gustav Klimt," *Who* 15),
"Long long I lay in the sands" ("A Vast Confusion," *Who* 44),
"Soon soon their supper will come / Soon soon they will eat it,"
"Soon soon they will devour each other," "Soon soon she will
finish eating / her appetizer / Soon soon she will look at him
again" ("The Astonished Heart," *Open* 14). The fact that all five
of the "Soon soon" repetitions just quoted occur on a single page
underscores the offense. The effect is heavy-handed, as though
the poet, aiming for what he has called "an algebra of lyricism"
("In Paris in a loud dark winter," *Pictures* #4), resorts to a mere
arithmetic of repetition. The repetitions are most effective when
the variant offers an element of surprise or unexpected elabora-
tion: "as if we did not know the music / as if we did not know
the melody" ("Seeing a Woman . . .," *Over All* 21); "The day
begins The day begins to end" ("History of the World: A TV
Docu-Drama" (9).[3] The latter example elegantly captures Ferlinghetti's recurrent theme of the concomitant pleasure and pain of
life.

The source of the weakness in these repetitions is the
attempt of the poet to steer his reader by means of artificial
emphasis. Several of his early poems are flagrantly guilty of
manipulative use of the words "real" and "really." Larry Smith
has tried to justify this "characteristic hip street talk lingo in the
'really' intensifier" (80), but such an explanation scarcely excuses
the abuse these words undergo:

> a real realist
> with a real tale to tell
> and a real tail to tell it with
> a real live
>   barking
>   democratic dog
> engaged in real
>   free enterprise. ("Dog," *Coney* 68)

The word "very" is forced to run a similar gauntlet in "They
were putting up the statue":

> a very tall and very purely naked
>   young virgin
> with very long and very straight
>   straw hair

and wearing only a very small
bird's nest
in a very existential place. (*Coney* 18)

Again, the intensifiers, without a doubt, are intended to be comic, but the inundation by repetition detracts from rather than enhances the humor. In similar fashion, Ferlinghetti tends to be unnecessarily didactic in presenting his materials:

thru the enormous meadow
which was the meadow of the world
....

thru the enormous meadow
which was the meadow of the world
("In Golden Gate Park that day," *Coney* 20);

The long street
which is the street of the world
("The Long Street," *Coney* 71);

inside the ultimate computer
which is the universe
("Rough Song of Animals Dying," *Landscapes* 54);

a condition ever desired
by tyrants
not least of which is
the great state.
("He with the Beating Wings," *Over All* 32)

In each instance the relative clause is poetically superfluous, as though the poet lacks confidence in the success of his presentation or distrusts the ability of his reader to understand his images. Ferlinghetti designs his poetry for communication on several levels. He aims for comprehension by the common people, the people of the street as opposed to those of the academy, but also incorporates materials intended to stimulate the cognoscenti: "I was always trying to write so that the poems could have a public surface which any one can get, but there's no reason it couldn't have another level which only the instructed can get" (quoted in Gleason). His didacticism seems to result from an insultingly low estimate of the intelligence of the former group.

Ferlinghetti's use of allusions is playfully and evocatively aimed at a more literate audience. Robert Peters has amusingly characterized the poet's approach as the "Norton Anthology School of Allusions" because of "the echoes of older poets, usually of their better-known lines (Ferlinghetti likes to echo Keats, Whitman, Yeats, Eliot, Pound, and Dylan Thomas)" (26) (surely one should also add Matthew Arnold to the list). However, Peters's humorous charge is an oversimplification toward an author who, even in his early poems, offers allusions to Djuna Barnes, Gertrude Stein, and Pietro di Donato (to mention only a few English language writers), authors who seldom appear on "Middle-Brow" reading lists. Indeed, his references to and echoes of acknowledged masters and less notable figures in the fields of literature, art, and music sometimes leave the impression of name-dropping; a similar weakness, geographical name-dropping, weakens a number of the poems in *A Trip to Italy & France* and *Over All the Obscene Boundaries*. His customary technique is to snatch familiar phrases or passages from popular works and to twist them for ironic purposes either through slight distortion or through altered context. Thus, in "Sailing thru the straits of Demos" (*Coney* 11-12), the Odyssean voyagers encounter surrealistic omens and promises of democracy; they set sail in a passage echoing lines 2 and 3 of Pound's Canto I, itself a translation from Book XI of Homer's *Odyssey*, providing a parallel to the idealistic quest—which is doomed to disappointment, anticipated by Ferlinghetti's irreverent substitution of "gobbly sea" for Pound's "godly sea"; the poem concludes as the travellers arrive at "the strange suburban shores" of America, where their response mimics that of the final lines of Keats's "On First Looking into Chapman's Homer," but with Keats's "wild surmise" reduced to "mild surprise." In a rather remarkable poem, "sweet and various the woodlark" (*Pictures* #27), allusion is central to the lyric's theme. There, the poet questions the validity of the verbal medium:

> But we have our own more recent
> who also fatally assumed
> that some direct connection
> does exist between
> language and reality
> word and world
> which is a laugh
> if you ask me.

However, the very existence and success of the poem in which these lines appear establish the connection which the poet, no doubt with tongue in cheek, denies. This is made even more emphatic by the next (and concluding) lines of the poem, which echo Shakespeare's *The Winter's Tale* (II.i.45):

> I too have drunk and seen
> the spider.

The allusion proves the power and efficacy of the verbal medium.

Ferlinghetti also offers frequent allusions to the works of the other Beat writers, particularly of Allen Ginsberg, whose major collections have been published by Ferlinghetti's City Lights Books. Ferlinghetti's involvement as editor for Ginsberg's poems has evidently impressed his fellow poet's materials upon him, resulting at times in rather peculiar effects. In Ginsberg's first volume, *Howl*, the passage "the empty lonely tincans with their rusty tongues alack" appears in the poem "Sunflower Sutra" (29). Thereafter, the last two words seem associated in Ferlinghetti's mind: "and shoe-tongues of roll-up shades alack" ("Euphoria," *Starting* 11); "among bent beer cans, rusted tongues alack" (*Mexican* 53); "with tongue alack" ("People Getting Divorced," *Who* 14). Ferlinghetti also playfully makes allusions to his own works: "Bashō would have liked / a lake like this" (*Back*) clearly echoes the opening line of "Dada would have liked a day like this" (*Pictures* #23); "Ah here's real proof / the soul has its rages—" ("The Man Who Rode Away," *Open* 34) refers back to "One could never tell / the soul has its rages" in "Autobiography" (*Coney* 63); "The force that through the red fuze / drove the bullet" ("An Elegy to Dispel Gloom," *Landscapes* 39) recalls Dylan Thomas's "The force that through the green fuse drives the flower" by way of Ferlinghetti's earlier adaptation of it in "Assassination Raga" (*Secret* 4).

Ferlinghetti employs language in an almost primitive sense, delighting in its playful possibilities. His allusions, puns, and word games illustrate this almost beyond patience. A problem especially arises when these devices detract from or supplant the poem. One often gets the impression that Ferlinghetti returns to his poems, seasoning them with allusions, slang, and verbal pyrotechnics. He has admitted to "doctoring them up. Hyping them up, might be more acccurate"

(Meltzer 154). Revision is not, of course, reprehensible in itself; however, the artist is at fault when the scars show, when the devices become so conspicuous as to be distracting, as Ferlinghetti's occasionally do. At times, as in "Don't let that horse" (*Coney* 29), a poem seems to be created simply for the sake of puns. At other times, a slang expression may be used so self-consciously that its occurrence is as irritating as chalk scraping on a blackboard: in "Sometime during eternity," Christ is described as "looking real Petered out" (*Coney* 16); in the same poem, the line "Him just hang there" originally appeared in *New Directions in Prose and Poetry 16* as "He just hangs there" (203). This revision may also show Ginsberg's influence, from his similar dialect usage in "America":

> Her wants to grab Chicago. Her needs a Red Readers' Digest. Her wants our auto plants in Siberia. Him big bureaucracy running our fillingstations.
> That no good. Ugh. Him make Indians learn read. Him need big black niggers. Hah. Her make us all work sixteen hours a day. Help. (*Howl* 33-34)

At other times, Ferlinghetti employs an effective game of verbal overlapping: thus, baseball, Eastern religion, and American politics combine in *Tyrannus Nix?* for "baseball Diamond Sutra" and "New Left Field" (9); a similar interweaving results in "pre-stressed Concrete poets" ("Populist Manifesto," *Who* 62). At their most successful, the verbal devices serve an integrating or digressive-progressive purpose. That is, the techniques lead the poet to consider a digressive thought which is then woven into the fabric of the poem and becomes an essential feature of its total design. Thus, in "Away above a harborful" (*Pictures* #1), the "morning sheets" hung out to dry, in the context of the "wind," "shrouds," and "kingdom come," become mourning sheets, winding sheets. Segovia's artistic profession lends the "bridge," "fret," "guts," and "Master Class" of "Moscow in the Wilderness, Segovia in the Snow" (*Secret* 40-48) a fully developed and legitimate ambiguity. The implicit comparison of a married couple and a pair of shoes allows the double meaning "mate," "sole"/soul," and "heel" of "People Getting Divorced" (*Who* 14) a wit-tempered poignance that escapes sentimentality.

In "Constantly risking absurdity" (*Coney* 30), Ferlinghetti both discusses and illustrates the elements of his poetic art. The poem begins with a focus on the poet as an entertainer:

Constantly risking absurdity
                    and death
        whenever he performs
                above the heads
                    of his audience.

Taking a theme parallel to Robert Frost's statement that a poem is "a performance in words," Ferlinghetti establishes a circus image, maintaining the perspective and values of the artist, for whom "absurdity," or not being taken seriously, is the most damaging threat. The line break after "performs" shows the poet's skill in following a pause with a qualification or modification of an apparently established notion.[4]   The introductory sequence could easily have ended after the third line: lines four and five reveal Ferlinghetti's concern about intelligibility to the masses, the common readers, while still conforming to the controlling image of the high-top. He goes on to describe the nature of the artistic performance:

            the poet like an acrobat
                climbs on rime
                    to a high wire of his own making
        and balancing on eyebeams
                    above a sea of faces
                paces his way
                    to the other side of day
        performing entrechats
                    and sleight-of-foot tricks
        and other high theatrics
                    and all without mistaking
                any thing
                    for what it may not be.

The assonance of "climbs," "rime," "high," and "wire" tightens the sound patterns of the lines, and the echo of sound in "climbs" and "rime" underscores the image in the line. The wire is "of his own making" as the poet, attempting to discover and embody his own voice, creates his own challenge. The "eye-beams" reflect the need of the poet for an audience and are also "I-beams," the subjective aspects of the poet's creation. The next two lines show a familiar Ferlinghetti technique of rhyming the last word of a line with the first word of the next line, a device he uses on several occasions:

> and I cannot sleep because of the thunder
> under the summer afternoon ("Euphoria," *Starting* 11);

> and hardpacks of Kents
> dents attesting to the passion.
>   ("Lost Parents," *Who* 12)

The true rhyme of "way" and "day" also carries on the assonance of "faces" and "paces," and "the other side of day" is the world of art, the world of darkness, of dreams, of danger, of images. The phrase "sleight-of-foot tricks," perhaps with a glance at Wallace Stevens's "The Sense of the Sleight-of-Hand Man," reveals the poet taking on a common phrase and altering it slightly to make it appropriate for the acrobat-on-a-high-wire image, but also for the poet performing his sleights on feet—metrical feet. The last lines of this section emphasize Ferlinghetti's obsession with accurate observation and with the dangers induced by the pathetic fallacy.

The next section of the poem develops the importance of the artistic role, with an allusive bow to Keats's Truth and Beauty:

> For he's the super realist
>   who must perforce perceive
>   taut truth
>   before the taking of each stance or step
>   in his supposed advance
>   toward that still higher perch
>   where Beauty stands and waits
>   with gravity
>   to start her death-defying leap.

The first line offers a glance at surrealism, the art of "the other side of day," and emphasizes, through the sound and structure echoes of "perforce perceive," again the need for the poet's clarity of perception. The Keats context of Truth and Beauty suggests that the "taut truth" may also be "taught truth," the indispensable tradition of past literary performers. The alliteration of "stance" and "step" and the rhyming sounds of "stance" and "advance" call attention to the deliberation of the artistic process. "Beauty" perches above the artist, ready to defy, in a multi-level pun, gravity, as well as death, in the Grecian-urn sense of immortality. The last section of the poem focuses on the very human artist:

And he
    a little charleychaplin man
        who may or may not catch
    her fair eternal form
        spreadeagled in the empty air
  of existence.

The Chaplin image of the bumbling but warm-hearted Little Man suggests the proletarian artist, engaged in an enterprise in which he may not be capable of success, yet daring it anyway, without the benefit of a safety net ("in the empty air") to save himself or his beloved Beauty. The poem finally stands as a testimony to Ferlinghetti himself. He attempts more daring tricks and steps than many of his contemporary poets, and, although he sometimes loses his balance along the wire, he advances toward and catches Beauty's form in the best of his poems.

Notes

[1]*New Directions in Prose and Poetry* 25 76. Ferlinghetti's notes were omitted when the poem was collected in *Open Eye, Open Heart* (96-108).

[2]In 1960 Ferlinghetti's City Lights Books published "The Naz" in Buckley's *Hiparama of the Classics* (14-17). A recorded version titled "The Nazz," originally recorded in 1951, appears on *The Best of Lord Buckley*.

[3]The passage in which this line occurs was omitted when the poem was collected in *Over All the Obscene Boundaries*.

[4]Inexplicably, several poems in *Over All the Obscene Boundaries* reveal a carelessness regarding line endings: "La Dame aux Camelias" (17-18) and "Plane Life" (110), for example, repeatedly conclude lines at normally weak articles, prepositions, and conjunctions—patterns which Ferlinghetti usually avoids.

List of Works Cited

Alvarez, A. "Introduction: The New Poetry *or* Beyond the Gentility Principle." *The New Poetry*. Ed. A. Alvarez. London: Penguin, 1966. 21-32.

Artaud, Antonin. *The Theater and its Double*. Trans. Mary Caroline Richards. New York: Grove, 1958.

Barth, John. *The End of the Road*. New York: Bantam, 1969.

Beckett, Samuel. *Three Novels: Molloy, Malone Dies, The Unnamable*. New York: Grove, 1965.

Brautigan, Richard. *Trout Fishing in America*. New York: Dell, 1972.

Breton, André. *Nadja*. Trans. Richard Howard. New York: Grove, 1960.

Brustein, Robert. *The Third Theatre*. New York: Knopf, 1969.

Buckley, Lord [Richard]. *The Best of Lord Buckley*. Elektra, EKS-74047, n.d.

—. *Hiparama of the Classics*. San Francisco: City Lights, 1960.

Charters, Samuel. *Some Poems/Poets: Studies in American Underground Poetry Since 1945*. Berkeley: Oyez, 1971.

Cherkovski, Neeli. *Ferlinghetti: A Biography*. Garden City: Doubleday, 1979.

D[oolittle], H[ilda]. *Palimpsest*. Carbondale: Southern Illinois UP, 1968.

Ferlinghetti, Lawrence. *An Artist's Diatribe*. San Diego: Atticus, 1983. N. pag.

—. *Back Roads to Far Places*. New York: New Directions, 1971. N. pag.

—. *A Coney Island of the Mind*. New York: New Directions, 1958.

—. *Endless Life: Selected Poems*. New York: New Directions, 1981.

—. "Genesis of *After the Cries of the Birds*." In *The Poetics of the New American Poetry*. Ed. Donald Allen and Warren Tallman. New York: Grove, 1973. 445-49.

—. *The Gunfather: Tale of the Cowboy.* Rev. ed. San Francisco: City Lights, 1981.

—. "Hairy Man." *New Directions in Prose and Poetry 17.* Ed. J. Laughlin. New York: New Directions, 1961. 132-33.

—. *Her.* New York: New Directions, 1960.

—. "History of the World: A TV Docu-Drama." *Evergreen Review* 98 (1984): 6-11.

—. "Horn on 'Howl.'" In *The Evergreen Review Reader.* Ed. Barney Rossett. New York: Castle, 1968. 134-38.

—. "The *Idiot* Interviews: Lawrence Ferlinghetti." *Idiot* 4 (1965): 8-11; 14-20.

—. *The Illustrated Wilfred Funk.* San Francisco: City Lights, 1971. N. pag.

—. "In a Time of Revolution for Instance." *Lemming* 1 (1971): 3-4.

—. "In a Time of Revolution for Instance." *New Directions in Prose and Poetry* 23. Ed. J. Laughlin. New York: New Directions, 1971. 44-46.

—. Interview. *Beef* 4.13 (December 1984): 4-5.

—. "Interview." With Lu Mezzetta. *Crusader* (23 March 1962): 3.

—. Interview. With Gavin Selerie. *The Riverside Interviews* 2. London: Binnacle, 1980.

—. "An Interview with Lawrence Ferlinghetti." With Andrei Codrescu. *San Francisco Review of Books* 3.5 (1977): 8-11; 35-38.

—. Jacket notes. *"Tentative Description of a Dinner to Promote the Impeachment of President Eisenhower" and Other Poems by Lawrence Ferlinghetti.* Fantasy, 7004, 1958.

—. *Landscapes of Living & Dying.* New York: New Directions, 1979.

—. "Las Vegas Tilt." *New Directions in Prose and Poetry* 25. Ed. J. Laughlin. New York: New Directions, 1972. 65-77.

—. *Love Is No Stone on the Moon.* Berkeley: Arif, 1971.

—. *The Mexican Night: Travel Journal.* New York: New Directions, 1970.

—. *Mule Mountain Dreams.* Bisbee, AZ: Bisbee, 1980.

—. "Museum of objects depicting the history of my race." *San Francisco Review* 1.2 (Spring 1959): 13-15.

—. *Northwest Ecolog.* San Francisco: City Lights, 1978.

—. *One Thousand Fearful Words For Fidel Castro.* San Francisco: City Lights, 1961. N. pag.

—. *Open Eye, Open Heart.* New York: New Directions, 1973.

—. *Over All the Obscene Boundaries: European Poems & Transitions.* New York: New Directions, 1984.

—. *Pictures of the Gone World.* San Francisco: City Lights, 1955.

—. *A Political Pamphlet.* San Francisco: Anarchist Resistance, 1976.

—. *Routines.* New York: New Directions, 1964.

—. *The Secret Meaning of Things.* New York: New Directions, 1968.

—. *Seven Days in Nicaragua Libre.* San Francisco: City Lights, 1984. N. pag.

—. "Sometime during eternity." *New Directions in Prose and Poetry 16.* Ed. J. Laughlin. New York: New Directions, 1957. 203.

—. *Starting from San Francisco.* New York: New Directions, 1967.

—. "Tall Tale of the Tall Cowboy." *New Directions in Prose and Poetry 45.* Ed. J. Laughlin. New York: New Directions, 1981. 1-2.

—. *"Tentative Description of a Dinner to Promote the Impeachment of President Eisenhower" and Other Poems by Lawrence Ferlinghetti.* Fantasy, 7004, 1958.

—. "Translator's Note." *Selections from Paroles.* By Jacques Prévert. Trans. Lawrence Ferlinghetti. San Francisco: City Lights, 1966. 3-6.

—. *A Trip to Italy & France.* New York: New Directions, 1981. N. pag.

—. *Tyrannus Nix?* New York: New Directions, 1969.

—. *Unfair Arguments with Existence: Seven Plays for a New Theatre.* New York: New Directions, 1963.

—. *Unfair Arguments with Existence.* New York: New Directions, 1963.

—. *Who Are We Now?* New York: New Directions, 1976.

Ferlinghetti, Lawrence, and Kenneth Rexroth. *Poetry Readings in "The Cellar" with the Cellar Jazz Quintet.* Fantasy, 7002, 1958.

Fiedler, Leslie. *Waiting for the End.* New York: Stein and Day, 1964.

Free [pseud. Abbie Hoffman]. *Revolution for the Hell of It.* New York: Dial, 1968.

Fuller, R. Buckminster. *Nine Chains to the Moon.* Carbondale: Southern Illinois UP, 1963.

Gall, Sally M. "Domestic Monologues: The Problem of Voice in Contemporary American Poetry." *The Massachusetts Review* 23.3 (Autumn 1982): 489-503.

Ginsberg, Allen. *Howl and Other Poems.* San Francisco: City Lights, 1956.

Gleason, Ralph J. Jacket notes. *Poetry Readings in "The Cellar" with the Cellar Jazz Quintet. Lawrence Ferlinghetti / Kenneth Rexroth.* Fantasy, 7002, 1958.

Ianni, L. A. "Lawrence Ferlinghetti's Fourth Person Singular and the Theory of Relativity." *Wisconsin Studies in Contemporary Literature* 8.3 (Summer 1967): 392-406.

Jarry, Alfred. "Exploits and Opinions of Doctor Faustroll, Pataphysician: A Neo-Scientific Novel." Trans. Simon Watson Taylor. In *Selected Works of Alfred Jarry.* Ed. Roger Shattuck and Simon Watson Taylor. New York: Grove, 1965, 157-256.

Kerouac, Jack. *On the Road.* New York: Signet, 1957.

Kherdian, David. *Six Poets of the San Francisco Renaissance: Portraits and Checklists.* Fresno, CA: Giligia, 1967.

Kirby, Michael. *Happenings: An Illustrated Anthology.* New York: Dutton, 1965.

Lautréamont, [Comte de] [Isidore Ducasse]. *Maldoror (Les Chants de Maldoror); Poésies.* Trans. Guy Wernham. New York: New Directions, 1965.

Lawrence, D. H. *Studies in Classic American Literature.* New York: Viking, 1966.

—. *Women in Love.* New York: Viking, 1960.

Lipton, Lawrence. *The Holy Barbarians.* New York: Grove, 1962.

Magritte, René. *Les amants.* Richard S. Zeisler Collection, New York.

—. *Le viol.* Menil Foundation Collection, Houston.

Meltzer, David, ed. "Lawrence Ferlinghetti." *The San Francisco Poets.* New York: Ballantine, 1971. 135-71.

Mueller, Janel. "The Mastery of Decorum: Politics as Poetry in Milton's Sonnets." *Critical Inquiry* 13 (Spring 1987): 475-508.

Peters, Robert. "Charlie Chaplin Between the On-Sale Sheets at Macy's." Review of *Endless Life: Selected Poems,* by Lawrence Ferlinghetti. *San Francisco Review of Books* 7.1 (1982): 25-26.

Poets of the Cities New York and San Francisco 1950-1965. [Dallas]: Dutton, 1974.

Prévert, Jacques. *Selections from Paroles.* Trans. Lawrence Ferlinghetti. San Francisco: City Lights, 1966.

Robbe-Grillet, Alain. *For a New Novel: Essays on Fiction.* Trans. Richard Howard. New York: Grove, 1965.

Rosenberg, Harold. *Art on the Edge: Creators and Situations.* New York: Macmillan, 1975.

Selerie, Gavin. *The Riverside Interviews 2: Lawrence Ferlinghetti.* London: Binnacle, 1980.

Serebnick, Judith. Review of *Her,* by Lawrence Ferlinghetti. *Library Journal* 85 (1 February 1960): 636.

Smith, Larry. *Lawrence Ferlinghetti: Poet-at-Large.* Carbondale: Southern Illinois UP, 1983.

Steiner, George. "Language Under Surveillance: The Writer and the State." *New York Times Book Review* (12 January 1986): 12, 36.

Stimpson, Catharine R. "The Beat Generation and the Trials of Homosexual Liberation." *Salmagundi* 58-59 (Fall 1982-Winter 1983): 373-92.

"The Swashbuckling Cut of a Cape." *Esquire* 76.1 (July 1971): 106-09.

Weiss, Peter. *The Persecution and Assassination of Jean-Paul Marat as Performed by the Inmates of the Asylum of Charenton under the Direction of the Marquis de Sade.* Trans. Geoffrey Skelton. New York: Pocket, 1965.

Whitman, Walt. *Complete Poetry and Selected Prose.* Ed. James E. Miller. Boston: Houghton, 1959.

Wilde, Oscar. *Complete Works.* London: Collins, 1966.

Yeats, W[illiam] B[utler]. *The Collected Poems.* New York: Macmillan, 1956.

Index